JOE GIBBS:
FOURTH
AND ONE

JOE GIBBS: FOURTH AND ONE

Joe Gibbs
with Jerry Jenkins

THOMAS NELSON PUBLISHERS
Nashville

To my wife, Pat,
and my sons, J.D. and Coy

Published in Nashville, Tennessee, by Thomas Nelson, Inc., and distributed in Canada by Lawson Falle, Ltd., Cambridge, Ontario.

Scripture quotations are from the NEW KING JAMES VERSION of the Bible. Copyright © 1979, 1980, 1982, Thomas Nelson, Inc., Publishers.

Library of Congress Cataloging-in-Publication Data
Gibbs, Joe.
    Joe Gibbs : fourth and one / Joe Gibbs with Jerry Jenkins.
    ISBN 0-8407-7660-8
    1. Gibbs, Joe. 2. Football—United States—Coaches—Biography.
3. Washington Redskins (Football team)—History. I. Jenkins, Jerry B.
II. Title.
GV939.G48A3   1991
796.332′092—dc20
[B]   91-24164
                                                                    CIP

Printed in the United States of America
2   3   4   5   6   7   —   96   95   94   93   92

Acknowledgments

I would like to thank the following people for their love and friendship and their influence on my life.

My family: Mom and Dad, my brother Jim, my Aunt Louise, and my late Uncle Walter, whom I loved.

The coaches I worked for: Don Coryell, John McKay, Frank Broyles, and Bill Peterson.

Redskins owner and my friend: Jack Kent Cooke, who made it possible for me to hire my first coaching staff: Don Breaux, Joe Bugle, Dan Henning, Billy Hickman, Larry Peccatiello, Richie Petibon, Dan Riley, Wayne Sevier, Rennie Simmons, Charley Taylor, and Lavern (Torgy) Torgeson.

My first general manager: Bobby Beathard—who gave me my chance.

And finally, my adviser Robert Fraley, my dear friend Don Meredith, my secretary Barbara Sevier, and my spiritual mentor George Tharel.

Contents

The Dream

If you've ever wanted something more than anything in the world, you understand how I felt when the rumors began.

I was forty years old and had been pursuing a head coaching job all my adult life. I had been an assistant for four major colleges and three NFL teams, but I had never had the head job anywhere, not even at a high school. It was all I wanted, all I thought about.

Now, rumor had it, head coaching jobs were pursuing me.

Gene Klein, owner of the San Diego Chargers (where I was offensive coordinator under Don Coryell), told me he had asked interested teams to wait until after the season to talk to me. That was only right; anything else was against the rules. But that didn't stop teams from asking my co-workers about me.

On one hand, I couldn't wait until the season was over to find out who was interested and how interested they really were. Was it possible I could become a head coach in the NFL after having been an assistant for so long?

On the other hand, the Chargers had just won their second straight conference championship, and like most everybody in Southern California, I believed we had Super Bowl potential. As offensive coordinator I enjoyed a lot of attention and credit for an offense that had Dan Fouts at

11

quarterback throwing to three all-pro receivers. Of course two other assistants, Ernie Zampesie (now with the Rams) and Jim Hanifan (now with the Redskins), deserve just as much credit. We seemed to break records every week, but I knew as well as anyone that Coryell was the key. He was the guy who would let me innovate and dream. If I looked good because of our offense, it was because Coryell gave me the freedom. We went into January of 1981 having beat Pittsburgh and won our conference, looking forward to the playoffs.

It was bad enough we'd had to play the Oakland Raiders twice during the regular season because they were in our division, but to have to meet them right away again in the playoffs . . . we looked awful. We jumped offsides five or six times, had a ball bounce out of a receiver's hands and into the defender's—stuff like that all day. That loss was a horrible, painful way to end a season, especially at home.

Coaches and players always feel like they're in the dumpster after a loss, but when you lose to a team you feel you should have beat and it finishes your season, you're really down. Not much was said in the locker room, though I had the feeling—the hope really—that I would not be coming back. I loved that team and the coaching staff, and I owed a lot to Don Coryell. He had given me my college football scholarship (half of one anyway) and later hired me as an assistant for three different teams. But I wanted a head job, and I could hardly wait.

It was late when I finally found Pat and the boys, J.D. and Coy (who were almost twelve and eight at the time), and our friends Rennie and Carol Simmons. We were all tired and somber as I drove north toward our home in LaCosta, stopping only for pizza.

I'd been told that someone might be calling me as soon as the Charger season was over, but I didn't expect the phone to be ringing when I got home that night. It was Bobby Beathard, general manager of the Washington Redskins.

"Sorry about the game," he said. "Tough way to lose."

"Yeah, thanks."

"Listen, we want to talk to you about the Redskins job."

"Sure, I'd love to."

"We'd like you to come to New York for an interview with the owner."

"Okay, great."

"My wife Christine and I are staying here in San Clemente. Why don't you come up here tonight and we'll drive to L.A. and fly to New York tomorrow?"

"When?"

"Tonight. Come on up tonight."

I looked at my watch. It was getting late. But, hey, I wouldn't sleep anyway.

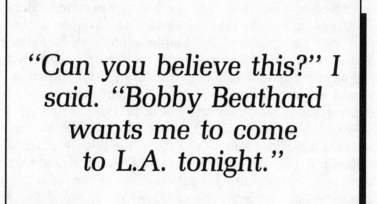

"Can you believe this?" I said. "Bobby Beathard wants me to come to L.A. tonight."

"Okay, sure."

I must have looked stunned. Pat didn't have to ask.

"Can you believe this?" I said. "Bobby Beathard wants me to come to L.A. tonight."

Over the years I'd had just two interviews for head coaching jobs—one at Arizona and one at Missouri—and in both places they had already decided upon someone else. As frustrating as not getting a head job was, not even being pursued was worse. I'd be a liar if I said it didn't feel great now to have the Redskins asking to talk to me.

The Simmonses dropped me off in San Clemente and

went back home, knowing how long I'd been waiting for this and how badly I wanted it. I rode on to Los Angeles with Bobby and his wife, Christine, and I got the clear signal from him that he was sold on me, even though the Redskins had beat us and our famous offense 40–17 just several weeks before. He advised me how to talk to Jack Kent Cooke, the flamboyant owner. I didn't know what to expect. I wanted the job and would have probably taken it on any terms, but I knew I would be in over my head with a man as powerful as Mr. Cooke. I was a jock, a football man, a lifetime assistant coach who had never made more than about $40,000 in any one year. I would be meeting with a man who had made hundreds of millions of dollars in media and real estate and sports teams.

I spent much of the night scribbling questions I didn't want to forget and areas we needed to cover, so when a fire alarm emptied the L.A. hotel for an hour or so, nobody had to wake me. After that I just stayed up, and early in the morning I went running with Bobby and Christine. I would get my chance to rest later. Right now I was too excited about the opportunity of a lifetime.

We took the earliest flight we could and checked into the Waldorf-Astoria in New York in the middle of the afternoon. Bobby preferred the casual look but thought a tie would be appropriate for introducing to the owner his choice for head coach. The cheapest tie he could find at the hotel was thirty-five dollars. "I'm not paying *that*," he said.

"Hey," I kidded him, "you go in there looking like a trash man, you're gonna get me fired before I get hired."

I went to my room to change into my best pin-striped suit, but I had hardly started when the phone rang. A gravelly voice asked if I was Bobby.

"No, this is Joe Gibbs."

"Joe Gibbs? This is Jack Kent Cooke. Welcome to New York."

"Thank you, sir. I'm looking forward to meeting you."

"Well, come on up."

"I'm just getting ready now."

"Well, you get up here right now."

"Yes, sir."

I hopped around getting that suit on, found Bobby, and said, "He wants us up there now."

Bobby went tie-less, but at that point I didn't care. I had my yellow pad with my questions and discussion topics. Mr. Cooke greeted us with a newspaper under his arm. He had a beautiful corner suite that looked out over the New York skyline, silhouetted against the darkening winter sky. He pointed to a deep, tufted chair. As I sat across from him I noticed his suit was perfectly tailored and his pocket hankie was folded just so. I had never felt more like a P.E. major.

I glanced at Bobby, who was silent and gave me a look that said I should be too. I waited. Mr. Cooke opened his newspaper and made an operation of finding the sports section. He held the paper wide open before him, hiding his face, and began to read aloud.

To me, in my frazzled state, it sounded like, "Blah, blah, blah, Gibbs, blah, blah, blah, genius."

Each time Mr. Cooke came to the word *genius,* he read it louder and more slowly than the rest, then stopped and pulled the paper down with a rattle so he could glare at me. He did that three times, and each time I felt a tingling in my seat and feared I would slide off the chair or be swallowed by it, which would have been okay with me.

Once he peered at me and said, "You know there were only two geniuses who ever lived."

One, he said, was Leonardo da Vinci. I don't remember the other, but I'm pretty sure it wasn't a football coach.

I didn't know what to say. *I* hadn't referred to myself as a genius. Some sportswriter had. If Mr. Cooke thought it was an overstatement, I'm sure it was. Meanwhile, I sat there hoping to somehow say the right thing or not say the wrong thing so I could get that job. At the same time, of course, I wondered, *What if I do get this job?*

When he quit reading the paper and we began to discuss my philosophy of coaching, what I would do with the team, and what I thought of Washington's potential, I was embarrassed. I had opinions, and I wasn't one to say only what I thought a man wanted to hear. But what a contrast! He was truly an intellectual. Widely read.

I'd say something, for instance, referring to San Diego, "Where I'm at now," and he'd say, "You mean, 'where I am now'?" And I'd say, "Yes, sir, where I am now."

I'd say something else and he'd say, "I don't think you really mean that. You mean. . . ." And whatever he'd say, I'd agree with, because I knew he was right.

When he asked what I thought it would take to do the job right, I referred to my list. I told him we needed a good film man because so much of post-game analysis depends on good film. I had a list of the coaches I wanted to hire. I wanted decent salaries for them, cars, moving expenses, meals provided when they worked late.

My hiring was not a foregone conclusion. I think he needed to be satisfied that I knew what I was talking about and that I had a plan. Bobby's recommendation carried a lot of weight, of course, but the conversation did not begin as if the decision had already been made. At one point Mr. Cooke turned and pointed out the window at the skyline.

"You recognize that building?" he asked.

"No, sir, I don't," I said.

"That's Jack Kent Cooke's Chrysler Building," he said.

And I had been worried about asking for too much money!

Before we got to that, I wanted to make sure I had covered everything on my list. I didn't want to surprise him later by raising some important item I had forgotten. There was a risk of appearing too demanding. But Mr. Cooke was ahead of me on most of my items, nodding as if they were natural requests.

I didn't know how to take him, but I could see it written all over him when he decided that I was his man. He had the look of a person hungry to succeed, to excel, to win. When I told him that most of the guys I wanted on my coaching staff were already working in the NFL and that they would be hard to get, he held up a hand and said quietly but forcefully, "We're going to get every single one of them."

If I had been excited before that, now I was really in gear. It was coming together. It was going to happen. I was going to become the coach of the Redskins.

More than salary, I was interested in exactly how the organization was built and where I fit in. "What's my role?" I asked Mr. Cooke. "Exactly what do you want me to do? I want to know what you expect."

He explained that Bobby and I would report to him. Bobby would get the players, with input from me and my staff. As general manager, Bobby would have final say on new players. I would have full responsibility for the coaches, the players once they were signed, the practices, and the games. I would have final say on which players stayed. Mr. Cooke would oversee everything, having final say on whatever he wanted.

Our last item of business would be dollars. I knew a salary of a little over a hundred thousand would be about right for a new coach, but I was prepared to ask for more. Of course, if he had insisted on half what I asked for, I would have agreed in a second. I never felt more out of place in my life, talking to Jack Kent Cooke about money. He was the one who raised the subject.

"What we need to talk about now is your salary. How would you feel about $110,000?"

I just stared at him. I wanted to be a big-time negotiator, but I was out of my league.

"What do you think you ought to make?" he asked.

That made it a little easier. I don't know how I got up enough guts to do it, but I said, "I think it ought to be $125,000."

Mr. Cooke didn't hesitate. "Well," he said, "I think $115,000 is fair."

"Yes, sir," I said. He had come up five and I came down ten, but at that point, I couldn't have been happier.

A lot of things have been written over the years about Jack Kent Cooke and his style, but I have to say my relationship with him has been great. He's a powerful and sometimes controversial man, but he has had confidence in me and let me do what he's paid me to do. That makes my job as close to perfect as it can get.

> ### *"Tell you what you do now,"* he said, *"you and Bobby go after all those coaches, and you get them."*

Eventually he stood, so I stood. We shook hands as he ushered me to the door.

"Tell you what you do now," he said, "you and Bobby go after all those coaches, and you get them."

Talk about your highs in life. It may sound silly to compare what I felt to falling in love, getting married, seeing your children born, or having an experience with God. But I was so high leaving that suite—knowing that I had not only finally landed a head coaching job, but also that it was in the NFL—that I could hardly function. I was not too old to be thrilled, to realize that this was a dream come true.

Here it is, the first time I ever get to choose and recruit and hire my own staff, and it's for a pro football team. Backed by the best owner in pro football, I can go after the people I want, offer them good salaries and great benefits, move them to the east coast, and provide them cars and meals when they're working. I'm not saying I wouldn't have taken the job if I had been able to negotiate only limited benefits or less money for my assistant coaches, but I was a guy who knew where his bread was buttered. I knew success would not rest on me. It would rest on getting the right coaching staff. By being able to offer them good packages, I knew we had a solid chance of getting every one of them. I was like a kid in a candy store, and I was so excited I couldn't sleep.

I mean I was wired.

Bobby would remember this better than I would, but I probably talked his ear off during our flight to Washington for a press conference. The conference was fun, thrilling really, but once I got there I was so excited I could hardly talk. Anybody who knows me knows that's rare! Here was an audience of reporters and I could barely get two words out.

I could not relax. I believe I didn't sleep for two straight nights. I made notes, talked things over with Bobby, and looked forward to talking personally to all the coaches I wanted to hire. They would all be at the Senior Bowl in Mobile, Alabama, the second to last stop on my fast tour from San Diego to LaCosta to San Clemente to Los Angeles to New York to Washington to Mobile and back home.

Most pro coaching staffs tried to get to the Senior Bowl. It wouldn't be long before the word got around that Gibbs got the Washington job and he's here recruiting assistants. One by one, the guys I wanted agreed to come, right down to the last guy. Coaches can't make a team win, but we were sure as heck going to do everything we knew to get the team prepared.

It seemed to me we had an organization that had a winning profile. We had good players and more to come, an owner and a general manager who wanted to win, and a town that had enjoyed good football but that wanted a real winner, a Super Bowl champion. I couldn't wait to get started.

Roots

People who know me know I'm an up-front guy, so let me tell you something early. I want this book to be more about life than about football, but I don't want to tell you my whole life story either. Because this is by me and about me, I know it's going to be sold as an autobiography. But I also know that not too many people outside my family care about my life story—and I'm not sure how many people *in* my family care either. What could be more boring than every detail about an ordinary American who eventually realizes his dream?

Now that you're into the second chapter and I've just told you that maybe you're not getting what you thought you paid for, I should tell you that there will be plenty of football here. In many ways, football has been my life. But I also have a few things I want to say about life, and in that you'll learn a few things about me without having to endure all the details of a fairly normal existence (until 1981). I promise to get from my childhood through college in one short chapter.

The lessons in my life have come from failures, my own shortcomings, naiveté, and buying into some of the biggest myths modern society has to sell. Maybe there's a lesson or two here that could help you avoid some mistakes. See, I bought into conventional wisdom, hook, line, and sinker. I mean, I believed I needed to make money, gain position and power and prestige (in my case that meant landing a head coaching job and winning), and accumulate things. If I accumulated enough, I would be happy. That was the picture. Everyone seemed to agree on it, and it looked right.

> *The lessons in my life have come from failures, my own shortcomings, naiveté, and buying into some of the biggest myths modern society has to sell.*

I also believed that people cared about each other. People are your friends, and they will help you in your quest for the top. If and when you become successful, you'll have even more loving, caring friends.

One thing I never could get comfortable with, however, was the idea that this is all there is. Besides money, fame, power, success, and loyal friends, society seemed to say that you have one life to live. You're young, so make the most of it because when you're through, it's over.

That myth never reached me; it never sank in and became part of my outlook. It's a good thing, because that one, especially along with the money and friends myths, will ruin you. It was the nagging knowledge that this life is *not* all there is that kept working on me, even during my frantic, frenzied years trying to embrace the other myths, that eventually made it possible for me to see my mistakes and get back on track. If that had never happened, I'd be one miserable man today. Because even if I had become the greatest coach in the history of professional football and had seen my teams win Super Bowl after Super Bowl, I'd have missed out on those few things that really are important in this life. That would have been a tragedy.

Oh, I was a slow learner. Even though I should have known better, I chased the American dream and almost caught it. Let me give you just enough of my background so you'll know where I was coming from and how I got to that day in New York, sitting across from Jack Kent Cooke himself, praying and hoping I was finally ready for the kind of a job I had been coveting most of my life.

Somewhere, people who don't know me get the idea that I'm sort of an intellectual type. Maybe it's the glasses. Maybe it's because I am comfortable in front of the press. In my immodest moments I'll even admit that maybe I have some pretty good football strategy. But don't put me in the same category as the widely-read professorial types. I'm basically a physical guy, not a reader. I read my Bible and the Matthew Henry commentary everyday, but I'm not one of those who reads much else. I like competition, racing motorbikes and cars, playing racquetball, that kind of thing.

I was a good athlete as a kid because I worked so hard at it. I had to. I wasn't one of those with natural speed and ability. I just loved all sports and was dedicated. All I did was play. My brother Jim and I grew up in the hills of North Carolina, mostly near Asheville, in the 1940s.

I loved that life. I was outdoors with my shoes off most of the time. We even went to school barefoot a lot. Some of my fondest memories are of sitting in tall grass with a shotgun, shooting birds and stuff.

My dad was a highway patrolman and then a deputy sheriff who moved us around. We didn't have much money, but still I felt spoiled. My mother, to protect us from Dad's drinking problem, let us run and play most of the time. I didn't have to do house or yard work and, if anything, my mother was liberal with us. She might bake a cake for us, and then she wouldn't limit us to one piece each. If we ate the whole cake, we ate the whole cake.

Because both my parents worked, I also spent a lot of time at my Aunt Louise and Uncle Walter's, my mother's brother. He was a great guy, a kid at heart with a creative, inventive mind. Like most everybody else around there, he worked at the Enka Rayon Plant, a textile mill. To me he was just Uncle Walter, the most fascinating guy in the world. He made us a soap box cart. He was also the first man in those parts to get a television. It had a huge antenna and a tiny screen. He and my aunt didn't have kids, so he spent a lot of time with us, making things in his basement, fixing radios, doing all kinds of things. He built us the fastest sled, and when the snow came we blocked off the roads and went sledding.

What a life we had! I wanted to be the best baseball, basketball, and football player ever. It seemed all our spare time went into playing. My dad set up a basketball backboard and hoop in our yard, and we spent hours there.

I can only guess that it was my lack of natural ability that made me so competitive. Nothing came easy for me. I had to work hard to excel, and I was willing. My dream was to play football for Sandhill High School. We would move to California before I got the chance, but that dream made me a much better than average sandlot player—or, I should say, freshly plowed field player. There was nothing more fun than running with that football over freshly turned earth.

Somehow I got in a fight with a bigger kid in our neighborhood, and I ran home. My dad made me go back and finish him off or be finished off. "Get your hide back over there," he said. I got beat up good. I learned a lesson: Don't start a fight unless you can win it, because if your dad is around, you'll have to finish it.

A vivid memory of my childhood is that I was often in the Enka Church. My mother, Aunt Louise, and my grandmother made sure I was there pretty much whenever something was going on. I was nine when I went forward to acknowledge that I believed in God. Even at that age and in that day I had heard all the stuff about life being accidental. A couple of things fused in a puddle of water millions of years ago, and now we wind up with men and women and the ability to love each other in a world like this? I didn't buy it. In church I learned that God made us, and He made us special. I believed He created the world, and it wasn't just because that made me feel better than the other theory did. It just made sense.

Even as a little kid I was fascinated by nature, and there was no way I could believe all the beauty and harmony and order just happened. That was my first big decision in life, and I never wavered from the basics of it: I decided that people, this earth, the Bible, all of it was done on purpose by someone who knew what he was doing. It was as simple as that. I went forward and prayed, "God, I know You're there. I know You made me." I chose to believe that, and I always have.

I also believed that the Bible itself was proof of the existence of God. It was written by more than thirty-five authors over 1,500 years, and still it's perfect. When I think of how one simple football play gets distorted when it goes from a coach to a player and then to the quarterback, I'm amazed that anything in the Bible fits together. Yet it all does.

I've come to learn over the years that the Bible—even the Old Testament—applies to me today. I'll be going through some crisis, wondering what in the world God would say about it, and I'll find not just a word or a verse about it but lots of different passages I can study and think about. It's amazing. It couldn't have just happened.

Joshua 1:8 says, "This Book of the Law shall not depart from your mouth, but you shall meditate in it day and night, that you may observe to do according to all that is written in it. For then you will make your way prosperous, and then you will have good success." If I had learned that as early as I had learned that God created me, I might not have had to learn so many of life's lessons the hard way.

My dad, Jackson Cephus Gibbs, was a big, generous guy everybody liked and watched out for. He always hated that name. The first thing he did when he was of age was to go to the courthouse and get his name changed to just his initials: J.C. He could make friends in an instant. If he was visiting a town, he would befriend the locals in half a day. He was transparent, a hundred-mile-an-hour talker, and everybody loved him. Once he was driving while under the influence and smashed through a neighbor's fence. The man came out with his shotgun, but when he saw who it was, he just said, "Oh, J.C., for Pete's sake!," helped get the car out, and drove Dad home.

He had grown up without a father and never finished high school. But he was always a good provider and treated my mother great. Dad was a tough, hard-nosed fighter type, defending his friends. He took care of the town and the town took care of him.

Dad's job depended on who was elected sheriff, and there were no guarantees past four years. He and my mother worried a lot about that lack of stability, and not long after Uncle Walter and Aunt Louise moved to California, we followed them out there. We settled in Santa Fe Springs near Whittier, where my dad eventually got a job in the legal department of the Bank of America.

It was 1955. I was about to begin high school, and it was a perfect time and place for me. I loved cars, hot rods, burger joints, girls, you name it. One of the first guys I met and played football with was a kid named Warren Simmons. We still call him Rennie. We have been friends ever since, and he's on my coaching staff today.

Boy, we had fun in high school! Friday night was the boys' night out, cruising and fooling around. No girls allowed. Saturday night was date night, and the romantic guys would also walk their girls to school or carry their books. That wasn't me. I got tired of most of my girlfriends after a couple of weeks, and I sure wasn't one to hold hands or carry books or hang around them all the time.

Then, when I was a junior, I noticed a sophomore cheerleader who was a dark-haired beauty. I still only dated on Saturday nights and I never walked her to school, but I still haven't gotten tired of Pat. We dated for almost eight years and we've been married more than twenty-five.

To admit that I was named Athlete of the Year when I graduated in 1959 makes it sound like I was better than I was. I think my advantage, for the award anyway, was that I loved the three major sports—football, basketball, and baseball—and was a starter in each. I was the quarterback of the football team, and my dream was to be a pro player, but I knew that was a long shot. I still had to work very hard to achieve anything. I still wasn't particularly big or fast, and there were probably better players than me on all those teams. I doubt anybody loved playing more than I did though.

After not getting a scholarship to a major university, I was pretty realistic about my future in football. I went to Cerritos Junior College where I desperately wanted to play quarterback. My high school coach must have told them I was more suited to center or tight end, because I was immediately switched to end.

I continued to play hard, and I got noticed, as all junior college players hope they will, by Don Coryell, head coach at San Diego State. He offered me half a scholarship and I jumped at it. I still wanted to be a pro, but short of that, I dreamed of returning to Cerritos J.C. as an assistant football coach. Pat and I talked about that a lot. We thought it would be fun to go back to the area where we met, get married, and settle in at a job I loved.

I played guard, tight end, and linebacker for Coryell, and I found him to be a brilliant coach. I loved his ideas and worked hard for him, trying to learn everything there was to know about offensive strategy, motivating players, working with people. If I couldn't play pro ball, I wanted to be a coach like Coryell. He noticed me too. Though I was only a half-scholarship guy from a community college, and though I wasn't monstrous or speedy, he knew I was dedicated. I always felt I knew what the coaches wanted. I did what I was told, and I did it as hard as I could.

The coach didn't know, of course, that when I was not

in training during the season, I was just about as much of a degenerate as most of the guys I ran with. We lived in a place called the Cave where friends came by and had lunch and threw papers all over the place. The windows were mostly broken out. We stayed up half the night at another place called the Farm, playing cards and drinking beer. Somehow I still maintained good grades. I knew that was important, but I even cheated in a few of my classes, I'm embarrassed to say. We were a bunch of rounders, fun-loving guys who weren't malicious but who were usually up to no good. I got in occasional trouble and had my share of fights. A couple of times I almost got kicked out of school.

The football types, the maniacs, the aggressive brawlers, those were my kinds of guys. My faith, what remnant was left of it from childhood, was pretty much a memory by then. I still believed there was a God and that He created the world and people, but right then it wasn't making any difference in my life.

Rennie Simmons and a guy named Wayne Sevier played on Coryell's team with me. Wayne coaches for me today, and his wife, Barbara, is my secretary. I believe in loyalty and long-term friendships, as much as I believed in staying in shape during the season and giving my all in practice as well as in games.

It paid off because when my playing days were over and I was a young married man in graduate school, Coach Coryell asked me to be a graduate assistant on the football team. Then I really started soaking up knowledge about what it took to be a coach. I still had my eye on a job at Cerritos, so doing grunt work for Coryell and his assistants, Sid Hall and a big man named John Madden, was worth it.

When a job opened at Cerritos for an assistant football coach, Pat and I eagerly drove back for an interview. I had a good shot at that job, and we were both excited. Pat especially wanted me to get it so we could move back home.

Just before the offer came, the line coach at San Diego

State—who had been there more than thirty years—re-tired. Almost casually, Coryell asked me, "Do you want to stay on and coach the line here for me?"

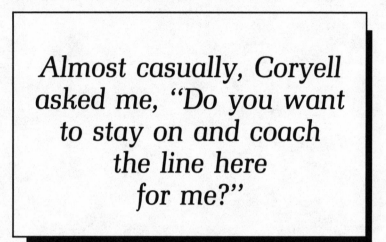

Almost casually, Coryell asked me, "Do you want to stay on and coach the line here for me?"

I wanted to move back home almost as much as Pat did, but I couldn't pass up an offer like that. Coaching line at San Diego State under Don Coryell? I had no idea what the future held for either him or me, but I knew this was a break. I accepted, and Pat cried all night. It wasn't that she disagreed with the decision; it was just that she had been excited about the other deal.

In 1966, that first year as an official coach on the staff, I saw San Diego State go 11–0 and win the national small college championship. In the three years I'd been helping out, we were 27–4. It was a great way to start a coaching career.

After that season I got a call from a man named Don Breaux (pronounced Bro), who spoke with such a thick southern accent that even a North Carolina native could hardly understand him. He was a fast talker, had heard good things about me somewhere, and wondered if I'd be interested in a job at Florida State University under Bill Peterson.

Bigger school. More money. Our first home. Pat, can we talk?

The Brass Ring

Twelve thousand dollars a year to be a university assistant football coach sounded like a fortune to me. And when a friend of the athletic department drove me to a new housing development and offered a brand new 1,800-square-foot home on a corner lot with landscaping and all for four hundred dollars down (you read it right) I looked in the windows and took it without even going inside. When Pat saw it, she wept with joy.

We had driven across the country in her 1964 Mustang, our only vehicle, stuffing it with necessities and shipping the rest. We stopped in Houston to visit our good friends Dave and Deann Stenson, and we also wound up buying a dog. We named him Beau Jack, and we had him for a long time. (Several years later I came home from work one night—actually in the wee hours of the morning—and knelt at the side of the bed to pray, resting my chin on the covers. Pat, roused from a sound sleep, was convinced it was Beau Jack, begging to get on the bed. "Beau Jack!" she shouted, kicking me in the face. "Stay down!")

At Florida State I coached under a wizard who was a little like a football Casey Stengle or Yogi Berra. Bill Peterson spoke in malapropisms, but he knew the game. Though he might call a close game a *cliffdweller* or say that he had good *repertoire* with his players, we knew what he meant.

It was during my two years there, while the Seminoles were going 15–4–1, that I got the bug to be a head coach. I saw young guys, colleagues, who were moving up the ladder, going from special teams coach to line coach to backfield coach to offensive coordinator and finally to the head job somewhere. That was where the action was. That was where I would find money and success and happiness. It became an obsession. I wanted to be a head coach.

I kept my eyes and ears open for opportunities, though I knew I was still too young and inexperienced, unless I was willing to drop a couple of divisions. I wasn't. When someone told me about an opening at the University of Southern California under John McKay, I immediately threw my hat into the ring. USC was big time, big name football. I would consider it a privilege and an opportunity.

> *That was where I would find money and success and happiness. It became an obsession. I wanted to be a head coach.*

Meanwhile, I had never really dealt with what had happened to my relationship to God. I had virtually ignored him during college, but still I went to church. Pat had been raised a Catholic, but she was not devout. While I was coaching at Florida State we attended a Protestant church in Tallahassee. Almost without my realizing it, Pat was becoming very intrigued with the idea of a personal encounter with God. I was in church because I knew it was the right thing, but my life was dedicated to getting ahead, chasing the brass ring. I wanted fun and action, money, success, and happiness; Pat, apparently, was ready for something deeper with God.

The church we attended often gave people the chance to give their lives to Jesus Christ, to ask forgiveness for their sins and invite Him into their hearts. One evening Pat up and walked forward. I'll tell you, spiritually she took off like a shot and passed me like a rocket. I mean, all of a sudden she was interested in her Bible, in talking to friends who know Christ, in spending lots of time with the people of the church. I was pleased that we agreed on something so basic and fundamental. I knew that putting Christ first in your life was the right thing to do, and I was barely aware that I was far from doing that. I'd been so busy getting ahead that I was putting God on a shelf except on Sundays.

I had other things to be excited about. We were expecting our first child. And I had been summoned for a meeting with John McKay at USC. I wanted that job so bad I could taste it. McKay and I talked for a long time, and at first I felt the meeting was not going well. He seemed too serious, almost negative. I tried to discuss strategy.

Somewhere in the conversation, I'm not sure when or why, I could tell that McKay had decided he wanted me. I knew there were several guys after the job, but here was McKay telling me, "Well, we'd really like you to consider joining our staff."

Consider it? I would make $14,000 if I stayed at Florida State. McKay was offering $13,200. I took it in a second. Pat and I sold our home (we got $2,000 down). We'd paid more than twice that for our first brand new car, a 1968 Olds Toronado, brown with a tan interior. I loved that car. After putting my very pregnant wife on a plane to California, I drove across country to the place I believed was a stepping stone to head coaching. I knew I was moving around quickly and often, but I was on a mission. As long as I kept moving up, I would keep moving on.

I was a better football coach than a first-time expectant

father. Pat had what I now know was a fairly typical first labor. Other couples came and went all day and half the night as Pat suffered through eighteen hours. The nurses kept telling me everything was all right, but all I knew was that the baby hadn't come yet. I hated to see Pat in pain. My blood pressure was rising, and I was telling the nurses —a new one with each shift—that no, everything was not all right. Something was wrong.

When the ordeal went past midnight, I started demanding to talk to the doctor. He wasn't there. He would come when he was needed. I needed him then. After having been called into the delivery room three different times and suffering all the trauma that goes with seeing your wife struggle and thinking you're about to become a father, I got fed up and went into the waiting room.

"I'm not going in there again," I said. "Don't come for me again until the baby's born."

When still nothing had happened after more than seventeen hours at the hospital, I demanded the doctor's home phone number. I had been getting messages throughout that he would know when to come. I told him, "I want you down here, and I want you down here right now."

"Well, I'm sure when the nurses think—"

"I want you here now! Do you understand what I'm saying?"

"Yeah."

He arrived at about four in the morning, and Jason Dean Gibbs was born twenty minutes later.

I have to confess that with one child in our family, my life didn't change that much. It should have, but I was still on the trail of the perfect job. That made me a tireless worker.

I was a good assistant coach, not only because I wanted to get ahead, but also because I really wanted to please the head coach. I couldn't work for a football program unless I was sold on it, because part of any assistant's job is selling the program to parents of potential players. I worked hard at recruiting, not to get ahead but to try and be the best representative I could for that program.

At USC I again found myself involved in a winning tradition. Over two seasons the Trojans were 15–4–1, just as Florida State had been when I was there. Naturally I like to think I had something to do with that and, looking back on it after more than a decade of NFL coaching, I know that being associated with winning programs had a huge impact on my future. Having been ferociously competitive all my life, I thrived on winning. What I wanted, still, was to be a university head coach.

Don Breaux, who had left for Arkansas before my second year at Florida State, called me in California to ask if I wanted to apply for the offensive line coach job at Arkansas. At first I wasn't sure. Leave USC? Head east again? Another assistant job? Admittedly, the head coach was the legendary Frank Broyles, the southern gentleman who has done color commentary on countless TV games.

"A lot of head coaches have come out of Arkansas," Don Breaux told me. That was all I needed to hear. After two seasons with USC I prepared to take my wife and two-year-old J.D. across country one more time. We sold our house in Huntington Beach to a real estate guy who assured me that I could go on ahead to Arkansas and Pat could supervise the loading of the moving van a few weeks later.

"I'll follow through with the paperwork and handle the closing," he said.

"How long will that take?" I asked. I wanted to get going. Pat was willing to wait around a few days while the movers emptied the house.

"Tell you what," Real Estate said. "I'll rent it from you for a couple of months, and then we'll close on it."

That sounded great to me. I was gone to Arkansas within hours, getting acquainted, moving up another run on the ladder toward head coaching. On moving day I got a call from Pat. She was nearly hysterical.

"He backed out," she wailed.

"What're you talking about?"

"They were putting the last piece of furniture on the truck, and he came by and said he'd changed his mind and wasn't buying the house."

"Let me talk to him!"

"He's gone. They took a chair off the van so I could have a place to sit." She was crying, and I could hear J.D. in the background. What a mental picture! My poor wife sitting in a lone chair by the phone in an otherwise empty house. I was furious.

"Just have someone get you to the airport and take the next plane back here," I said. "We'll just have to hope and pray that it sells."

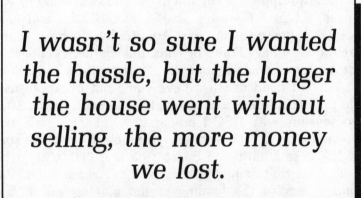

I wasn't so sure I wanted the hassle, but the longer the house went without selling, the more money we lost.

My dad went nuts when he heard that story. Here he's doing legal legwork for the high-powered attorneys of Bank of America—investigations, serving papers, that kind of stuff—and he knows enough about the law to know this guy shouldn't get away with how he treated us. We had been naive, sure; we should never have trusted someone we hardly knew. But even oral promises are binding, so my dad had papers filed on the guy in court. "We're gonna get him," my dad said.

I wasn't so sure I wanted the hassle, but the longer the house went without selling, the more money we lost. Eventually it sold, but for a couple of months we had to pay two mortgages, and we lost out on the rent the guy had promised.

About a year later, when Pat and I were back in California for a vacation, the court date came up and my dad took us to the courthouse with a friend of his. The friend happened to be one of the top lawyers for Bank of America. I mean, he looked, sounded, and acted the part. The other guy, who was too embarrassed to even look at us, had some local kid representing him who looked like he'd just got out of law school.

The attorneys were called to the bench and the judge said, "How long do you think this will take?"

The young lawyer said, "About fifteen minutes, your honor."

Our lawyer smiled and said softly, "Judge, our case alone will take three hours to present."

"What?" Youngster said.

"I'll schedule this for later on the docket," the judge said.

Our lawyer immediately turned and gathered up his stuff, as if this was what he expected. We followed him out into the hall, and here came the other lawyer. "We'd like to settle," he said.

Our lawyer told us we could have hit him for the rent and a few thousand more for the inconvenience and all that, but I said all we wanted was the two months' rent. We had that check before we left the courthouse. Live and learn. I had never claimed to be a legal or financial wizard, but I should have taken a lesson from that debacle.

As usual, I was having a great time coaching the offensive line. Except for becoming a head coach, I couldn't imagine wanting anything more from life. I was getting paid to be involved with a sport I loved. I traveled all over the country recruiting players. We had a little boy and another baby on the way. Life was good. We lived in Fayetteville and were attending the First Baptist Church. I was even enjoying that more than I thought I would.

Church had been an obligation for me for several years, but now with another baby on the way and my thirtieth birthday a memory of almost two years already, I was starting to think more seriously about life. My heart still burned after a head coaching job, and I was still as fiery and competitive as ever, but I had begun thinking about what kind of a person, what kind of a father I really wanted to be.

J.D. was toddling around, talking, developing his own personality. I knew it wouldn't be long before the new baby would be at this same stage, and J.D. would be almost ready to start school. These babies didn't stay babies for long. They became children, kids, people. Pat had known that all along, but I had been almost too busy to notice. It wouldn't be long before we would be a family of four. Not just two adults and two babies, but four people who needed to know how to interact and communicate with each other. My actions would impact my kids. They wouldn't always see me as a curiosity who was here some days and gone others. They would care about me, wonder and know where I was, see how I lived. I was almost thirty-two, about to become a father again, and I was starting to grow up.

Major changes were in the wind for me, but I didn't know it. They were sneaking up on me.

George

I've never worked with products or goods. My whole life has been people. I've either recruited them to play ball for me at colleges or with the Redskins, or I've tried to hire them to work with me on a coaching staff. I've analyzed, decided, and wooed people, then tried to mold them into a unit. I like people.

I find people's lives interesting. It's exciting to find out how people got where they are in life. I like to know how and why they make decisions. And people have had tremendous influences on my life. I watch them, study them, and when they are admirable, I try to learn from them.

I'll never forget the first time I worked with Raymond Berry, the legendary Colt receiver who set many records in his career. He's an outstanding believer in Jesus Christ, brutally honest, a straightforward guy who relates well to people.

He and I were on Frank Broyles's staff at Arkansas, doing some hard recruiting in the off-season. You have to know this recruiting game. I enjoyed it and worked like the dickens at it. It's a challenge, but it's also an art and not a science. You make calls, write letters, visit, schmooze with parents, and try to keep the kid warm until you've fully qualified him. Only certain players fit with certain universities. We looked for a specific type of kid at Arkansas, and until we determined that a kid would not

45

fit, we had to keep him from signing with someone else or
getting turned off to us. You have to know how much to
stay in contact and when to leave him alone. Some parents like lots of attention, and some get tired of it very
quickly.

Raymond Berry came to the Arkansas coaching staff
from the Dallas Cowboys, and he was new to college
recruiting. He was fresh and optimistic, and most of all he
believed what people told him. In a meeting with his
recruiting coaches, Frank Broyles went around the room
asking each of us where we stood with certain prospects.

"Joe," he said, "how do things look in Houston?"

"I'm visiting twelve kids," I said. "I'm hoping to get
three or maybe four of them."

That was fairly typical of the other veteran coaches.
They knew that kids will tell you one thing and do another, and so will their parents. The fact is, we coaches
did the same. We wouldn't tell a kid we were going to give
him a scholarship and then not do it, but if we knew a kid
wanted to be a receiver and we already had plenty, we
wouldn't say much about the fact that he might wind up as
a defensive back for us.

We had a great passer in Joe Ferguson, so receivers
wanted to play for us. You can only have so many, so
while we were talking up what a great quarterback we
had, we were evasive about any guarantees that the kid
would be a receiver. I'm not saying it's right. I'm just saying that's how it's done, and that was how I did it in the
spiritual state I found myself in 1972.

Frank Broyles got to Raymond and asked him how he
felt about his upcoming trip to Dallas. "Great," Raymond
said. "I'm visiting eleven kids and I think I'm going to sign
them all."

Heads shot up all over the room. Some of us laughed.
Eleven out of eleven? How could anybody be so naive?
Raymond was so innocent and honest and trusting that he
believed all the players who told him they would sign. We
all knew the kids would be attracted to a Hall of Famer
like him, but nobody signs eleven out of eleven!

"Raymond," someone said, "are you crazy?"

"No," he said, "really. Most of these kids have told me that they're coming." Raymond tells people the truth, so he expects them to do the same. He was such a great guy that we found him admirable. At least I did. Admirable, but naive.

We headed out for our recruiting visits and I arranged for Raymond to come to Houston after his Dallas trip. I was working on a couple of receivers; I'll call them Brian and Reggie. I wanted them both, and they both said they were coming. I had spent a lot of time emphasizing Joe Ferguson, and I thought letting them meet a great like Raymond Berry would really ice it.

Well, he shows up with me at Brian's house, and the first thing he does is whip out a yellow pad and say, "I just want to tell you something right away. From the kids it looks like we're going to get, there's a chance you're going to have to play defensive back."

I could have killed him. I saw the kid's face cloud over, and I jumped in and suggested we go out and get something to eat. I didn't know Raymond was already sold on Reggie. And I certainly wasn't about to try to recruit a receiver by telling him he was going to have to play DB.

We got Reggie. We lost Brian. On signing day, I had four kids who followed through on their promises. Not one of Raymond's eleven hopefuls from Dallas signed. He was crushed. We gave him some good-natured razzing, and he learned a tough lesson the hard way. He became a good recruiter, and of course went on to become an NFL head coach, leading the New England Patriots into the Super Bowl in 1985.

Despite my frustration with him over that recruiting disaster, I was deeply influenced by Raymond. He had such a peace about him that he commanded respect. He was soft-spoken and his players listened to every word. He was self-effacing and gentle. I have to admit it; I was an egotist. I was rigid. I wanted my own way, and I didn't have much time for people who disagreed with me. Raymond was the opposite. I didn't let it show, but his life was working on me.

Once at practice, one of Raymond's receivers dropped a pass and Frank Broyles, from his perch in the stands, hollered at the kid. I could tell Raymond didn't like it. He wanted to coach his player his own way, and ridiculing him for a mistake was not Raymond's way. A few minutes later, the same thing happened. Raymond turned and glanced up at Coach Broyles.

When it happened yet again, Raymond said quietly, "I'm going to have to talk to Frank about this."

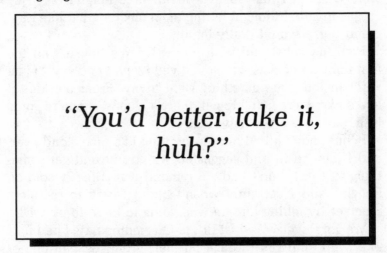

"You'd better take it, huh?"

I nearly laughed. What was he going to do, tell the head coach he shouldn't holler when he wanted to? Raymond went to Frank and they talked briefly. I don't know what was said, but there were more dropped passes and no more shouts from Frank. Frank Broyles is a man of quality character too, so he would know how to respond to an approach like that from Raymond.

When Raymond was moving away from Arkansas, he put his expensive home up for sale in a depressed market. He got an offer for ten or fifteen thousand less than he wanted, and I said, "You'd better take it, huh?" I was transferring my own eagerness and nervousness to him.

"No," he said. "I don't feel led to take that offer."

He didn't feel *led?* I admired his tranquillity, but I didn't understand. Fayetteville was such a small town that not too many people moved in there with that kind of money. A few weeks later he got the price he wanted.

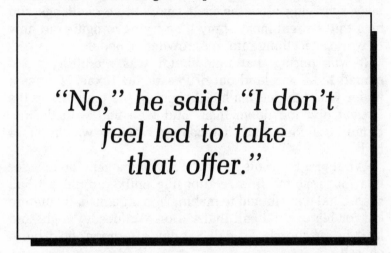

"No," he said. "I don't feel led to take that offer."

Don Breaux was another coach whose life had an impact on mine. He'd been a lot like me at Florida State. Now two years later he was like a different person. He had a fresh outlook on just about everything. His language was clean, his relationship with his wife and kids was special. I knew no one could change his life-style on his own. I finally asked him, "Don, what is it with you?"

"I've made a commitment to Christ, Joe," he said. "I gave my life to him and he's totally changed me."

That made me think. I considered myself a believer. I *was* a believer. I believed since I was a child. I knew there was a God and that He had made me and the world and everybody else. But that was pretty much the extent of my faith. Pat and I attended the First Baptist Church of Fayetteville, again because I knew it was the right thing to do. She was still new and serious in her own commitment, so she was much more into it than I was.

I was intrigued by the adult Sunday school class teacher, a small, older man named George Tharel. Again, it was as much his life as his teaching that reached me. He was a man at peace with himself and with God, and of course that made him a man at peace with other people, too. Being driven was one of my strengths, but I envied people who could relax and enjoy life, enjoy God. I was so busy scurrying after the next competitive challenge and high that I spent most of my time trying to figure out how to work everything into my crowded schedule.

It was during that time that I was recruiting a kid named Mike Kirkland out of Pasadena, Texas. He was a junior who had led his high school to the play-offs in the biggest division down there and who had won the national Pass, Punt, and Kick contest when he was in junior high.

What great parents he had! They had a genuine love for him that resulted in a relationship unlike anything I had seen. That contributed to making him an unusually mature kid for his age. I'd call that kid on Wednesday night and he'd be in church. I'd call Sunday afternoon, he'd be in church.

About six months into the recruiting process, it came out that he was adopted. I don't know why that surprised me, but it did. His father was so proud of him that he enjoyed showing me his old trophies and ribbons and records. This wasn't a case of a father living his own dream through his son; it was more simply a father with great love.

Mike's mother was also impressive. She was always honest with me. I'd have a great meeting with them and feel I'd made progress, and she would always say as I was walking out, "You know, Mr. Gibbs, I need to tell you I'd rather have him go to Baylor."

That hurt. It was understandable, because they lived in Texas and they were Baptists, but still it hurt. When I was ready to make my final pitch, just before commitment time, I said, "Chances are if he goes to Baylor, he's never going to get to play in the Cotton Bowl." (Two years later, Baylor was in the Cotton Bowl. How could I know?)

I also assured them they would enjoy the nine hour drive up to Fayetteville, through the beautiful mountains and trees. (We signed Mike, but every time I saw Mrs. Kirkland after that, she said, "By the way, that drive is eleven and a half hours.")

I was more impressed than I can say with that family. It was obvious they each had a wonderful relationship with God and with one another. It gave them great unity and a beautiful life together. That's what I wanted. I wanted to be that kind of a father and have that kind of a family. I knew Pat wanted it too. I was the odd man out. If our family wasn't like that, I would be the reason.

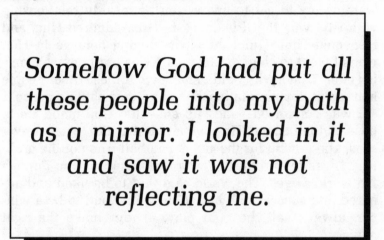

Somehow God had put all these people into my path as a mirror. I looked in it and saw it was not reflecting me.

Another of the assistant coaches at Arkansas was Paul Lanham. He and his wife Helen had a fantastic family for the same reasons as the Kirklands. It seemed everyone in their neighborhood wanted to spend time at their home because it was such a happy, joyous, peaceful place.

Somehow God had put all these people into my path as a mirror. I looked in it and saw it was not reflecting me. They had what I wanted, but I was not what they were. I believed in God, but I was not committed to Jesus Christ. They were, and that made all the difference. I was living by the world's standards, and except for not having yet landed the job I wanted and thought I deserved, I was measuring up. The problem was that though measuring up to the world's standard brought some success and even

some physical comfort and enjoyment, it was not success
on God's scale. My success was empty, and I was not
happy.

What was it about these people and their relationships
with Christ that made them so at peace? My Sunday
school teacher was saying that too many people, even
those who believe in Christ, don't understand that He
loves them even when they make mistakes. I believed that
He had made me special, that I was no accident, but
somewhere along the line I missed the part about His
wanting me to get to know Him better. My relationship
with God was that I believed in Him, admired Him, and
respected Him. I thought I was paying homage to Him
when I went to church. Fact was, I was pretty much ignor-
ing Him. That's why I didn't have what these other people
had: great, loving relationships, and that baffling peace.

I was convinced—and still am—that God made me to
be a football coach. He gave me desire, fire, competitive-
ness, and a mind for the game. Football was not the problem. I was the problem. I was looking at my life through
the world's eyes. The world said that to be liked and admired and successful, I had to do well. I had to be a winner, always call the right play, always make the right
move.

God was trying to impress upon me that in His eyes, I
was forgiven and loved no matter what. He wanted to
show me that His love would feel more real to me in the
bad times than the good, because that was when I needed
Him most. In the bad times, the down times, He would be
molding me and shaping me in the way I needed, knocking
off my rough edges to make me the kind of man He
wanted me to be. I could actually be advanced and improved through life's adversities, if I would commit myself
to God.

One thing I had become aware of was that I had not
been living for God. I had been living for myself. Here I'd
been chasing all these things I thought were important,
and I had been missing the point of life. The only thing I
was going to leave on this earth was what I poured into

my son and the baby that was on the way. Yet my biggest concern was whether I'd ever become a head coach. Don't get me wrong. That wasn't a bad goal. But for it to be the end-all mission in my life was certainly backward. I thought a job like that would make me a better person: successful, comfortable financially, respected, loaded with friends.

The kind of people I looked up to were macho men, bike and car racers, football players, people who knocked other people down and made their own ways in the world. Now I found myself drawn to a little Sunday school teacher who was a musician and a reader. George Tharel was a pillar of the community, the manager of the only Penney's store in northwest Arkansas. I couldn't help but respect him. He was a quiet, peaceful, loving man who clearly was trying to walk with the Lord and please God.

I talked to him more and more after class each week. He always had time for me and a good word too. The more we talked and the more I thought about all the other people God had put in my life that year, the more I knew I had been heading down the wrong road. It was time to get things straight. I needed to rededicate myself to Christ. I didn't talk to George about it. I didn't even talk to Pat about it, though she says now that she could see changes in me and knew it was coming. Most of this was happening in my own mind and heart.

As I sat in church one night, I felt God really working on me. I had not been living the right kind of life. I knew that living right was not what got anybody into heaven. Only the work of Christ could do that. But I wanted more than just assurance that I was going to heaven. I wanted to please God. I wanted to know Him. I wanted to be a person who was loving and at peace with his family. I wanted to be a man who had something to offer his children. It was time to live by God's standard rather than the world's.

I prayed silently in that church pew, telling God I was ready to commit myself to Him, something I should have done when I had received Christ as a child. Then I went forward to make a public statement that I meant business with God. My relationship with George Tharel deepened to the point where now, years after I left Arkansas, I still consider him my spiritual father. I hear from him nearly every week by phone or letter, encouraging me and admonishing me to continue my daily relationship with the Lord.

I felt a great weight lift from my shoulders when I rededicated my life, but no one told me life would get easier. I had more joy and happiness, but it's a good thing no one made that rash and incorrect promise. If anything, my life became more difficult after that. If someone were to use me as an example of what happens to a believer when he gets back on track with God, he might find people running the other way.

To say my life has never been the same would be an understatement. To say it's all been easy and happy would be a lie.

St. Louis

God had a lot of work to do in my life. He still does. But I began gradually growing. One of the things God does, I think, is something that shows His sense of humor. Rather than sending lightning or an angel or something to tell you you're self-centered, He simply lets you see it. He uses His Spirit to convict you.

I would find myself in an argument or disagreement with another coach, and suddenly I would be aware of how ugly I sounded. That had never crossed my mind before. I knew I had been self-centered and even a bit of a know-it-all, because people had said so. But then, hey, I was probably right—at least in *what* I said if not in how I said it. But now, God was active in my life. I saw myself for what I was. Too strong. Too rigid. Too self-righteous. Too self-centered. If this kept up, I would have to start going back to people I'd worked with before and start apologizing. It wasn't a pretty picture, but the more I saw it, the more I changed.

Two weeks after my thirty-second birthday I found myself in Houston rounding up fifteen or sixteen football players who were to fly back to Arkansas with me. It was December 9, 1972, and I was awakened at six in the morning by a call informing me that Pat was in labor and going into the hospital. Needless to say, that made it difficult to concentrate on the players I was responsible for. I had to take care of them, but all I really wanted to do was to get back in time to be with Pat.

We left at seven in the morning but got snowed in at Fort Smith. We were not going to get to Fayetteville anytime soon. I called the hospital from a phone booth. "Give me the waiting room for having babies," I said, knowing there had to be a simple term for it.

The phone rang and rang. Finally an old man answered with a deep Arkansan drawl. "Hello?"

"Hello, this is Joe Gibbs. My wife's there and supposed to be having a baby."

"Whadja say yer name was, son?"

"Gibbs."

"Gibbs?"

"Yes, sir."

"I think they already done had that baby."

"Really?"

"Yes sir."

"What was it? Do you know?"

"I believe it was a boy."

"Yeah? How big?"

"Jes' a minute." He turned away from the phone. "How big was that Gibbs boy?" He came back. "Ten pounds, Mr. Gibbs. Congratulations."

That was probably someone's grandpa, and I think he got a kick out of giving me the news.

Having two boys only doubled my sense of responsibility. I knew that being a parent would be one of the most important things I would do on this earth. I knew I would leave to these two boys my name and my legacy, whatever that would be. What did I want their lives to say about me? What kind of person would I be now?

Well, sad to say, in spite of my rededication and my resolve, I did let other things stay in the way of my being the kind of a parent I should have been when the kids were young. Some things were changing in my life, like how I acted with other people, my personal relationship with Christ, that kind of a thing. But I was still pretty naive about what it meant to be the right kind of a father. If I had it to do over, I would have been home more, even when the kids were real little. I know now how important that is. But back then I was still chasing dreams, trying to get ahead. My motives had been purified, but my priorities were still not where they needed to be.

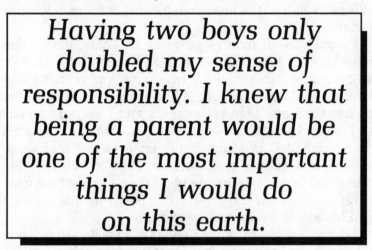

Having two boys only doubled my sense of responsibility. I knew that being a parent would be one of the most important things I would do on this earth.

At the end of the second football season at Arkansas, I knew I had to get out of offensive line coaching if I was ever going to position myself to be a head coach. I talked to Frank Broyles about it, and he agreed to let me become the defensive coach. Then I got a call from Don Coryell with an offer I shouldn't have refused.

"I've just been named head coach of the Cardinals," he said. "How about coming with me to St. Louis? I want you to coach the offensive line."

Here I couldn't get a university head coaching job and now I was wanted in the NFL. I should have had my head examined, but I almost turned it down. "Tell you what, Don," I said. "I appreciate it. I really do, and I'd love to coach in the pros. But I'm tired of coaching the line. I think I'd better stay here and coach on defense."

For a couple of days I was kicking myself. Turning down the pros. Man, what an idiot! Then Coryell called back. "I got somebody else to coach the line. How about coming and coaching the backs?"

He offered a darn good deal, but that was less important to me than working under Don again and getting to be a pro coach. The idea of coaching the backs was great too. The next step should be offensive coordinator, and that was the customary stepping stone to head coach. I was still thinking college head coach, but my horizon had just expanded.

I would coach for five years at St. Louis, longer than anywhere I'd ever been. From 1973 through 1977 we were 42–27–1, and I solidified my friendship and working relationship with Don Coryell. While there I got hooked first on handball and then racquetball, and I played as much as I could. I practiced before work, played over the lunch hour, competed in tournaments on evenings and weekends. I was getting good, and I craved the competition. The game began to grow on me. I didn't know how much of my life it would take over. All I knew was that I loved it and it seemed everyone else did too.

When I really got serious about it, I started to move up the ladder in the local club. Once I turned thirty-five late in 1975, I began competing in the thirty-five-and-older tournaments. I had found a passion that consumed me. I drove all over the country for tournaments and quickly realized I had a shot at the national title. Because I'd stayed in shape, I didn't play like a man my age or older. And because of the freedom my job allowed, I had the time to really infuse myself in the sport.

Meanwhile, I became convinced of the financial potential of the sport and became enamored with the idea of investing in it. A few friends and I would put up the initial money for a racquetball court, and we would all get rich together. I was certain of the deal. Pat was not.

I never wanted to ignore Pat's input, but I didn't want to be hampered by it either. Rather than cross her will or ignore her, I badgered and cajoled and sold her. I found a way to make her give in. When she said, "If you have to do it, do it," I took that as agreement and permission, and

I jumped in. Her real counsel and her true feeling was, "No, we shouldn't do this," but that's not what I heard. I heard what I wanted to hear, and soon after the first club was up and running, the group invested in another.

Every day I was up early in the morning, hitting balls for an hour and fifteen minutes. In the afternoons I would play singles against some of the better, and younger, players in the club. In fact, five of the best players in the world were in St. Louis, and I begged them to play me as often as possible. One of them was a fifteen-year-old kid named Marty Hogan who went on to become the best player in the world. He and I became friends and traveled to tournaments together. In fact, he learned to drive in my car. I remember the day he said he was going to be the best. I thought he was crazy, but he proved me wrong. I knew that could only raise my ability level. I was not a great athlete, but I was quick and had good eye/hand coordination. I was in decent shape and was semi-ambidextrous, so I was in a sport that was made for me.

I not only drove to tournaments now, but I also flew to some. The better I did in state and regional tournaments, the brighter my future looked on the national scene. I loved it. It was a great experience. It simply cost me something I can never go back and replace: time with my kids when they were little. What a fool I was. What a price I paid for the national championship in 1976! I know it was only the national seniors title, but it was a big deal to me. It was exhilarating. The sport satisfied a lot of needs I had: to compete and to excel and to win. But I was a jerk. I left Pat with all the work, and with all the joy of seeing the boys grow and develop. It isn't as if I wasn't there at all, but what was I doing? For some men it's golf that takes them away from their families. For me it was racquetball.

I was a better man than I had been, but boy, I sure had a lot more to learn. I finished second in the nation in 1977, but as I sat at a big tournament in Detroit, I got thinking. "I'm an idiot. Here I am running around the country to these racquetball tournaments, and my family is back home. That's it. I'm flying home after this. That's the end of it. I'm not doing this anymore."

Though winning that national title was one of the greatest and most fulfilling experiences of my life, it was selfish. If I could do it again, I would not charge around doing that when I could be home. Thankfully, from that time on, I had a great time helping raise our kids. We had many fun and humorous times, some good times and some rough times, but I wouldn't trade them for anything. I just wish I had those early years to live again.

Pat likes to put pictures of the boys on the mirror so I can think of them when I'm shaving. She changes the pictures occasionally, and it always hurts when she puts up old ones, when the boys were little and I wasn't there much. Those pictures almost make me want to cry. I should have been there. At least I discovered my mistake when I was in my late thirties and not older. I can thank God for that. Both boys were still under ten when I came to my senses.

I never became a perfect father, and I've never met one. But I did learn that showing your kids that you love them and care for them will overcome the mistakes you make as a parent. I always wanted my kids to know how I felt about them deep down. My occupation has given me lots of time with them, particularly in the off-season. The kids have skied and raced bicycles and been involved in every sport they wanted. We've had jet skis and motorbikes and all the other things they thought were fun. Most of all, once I got my priorities straight, we spent a lot of time together.

Being the sons of a jock, they became very physical and sports oriented. Pat jokes that we don't respect or care about any males who are not competitive. "In other words," she says, "if they don't like football, they're wimps. Let's kill 'em."

I hope it's not that bad, but it is true that in the third grade we heard from J.D.'s teacher that she was worried about him. "Everything in his life is physical," she said. "It's black and white, competition. Doing. Running. Competing. There's no music appreciation, no art appreciation. He's one-dimensional."

I got feeling bad about it. I mean, the kid was smart. School always came easy to him. He had pretty much taught himself to read in a few days when he was five, badgering Pat to help him with certain words. I thought he was doing okay. Now I felt guilty. I knew this problem was all because of me. I liked waterskiing and snow skiing, riding motorbikes, all that.

That evening I sat him down and I said, "J.D., I have a little concern here." I told him what the teacher said about our not giving him enough of a rounded view of life.

"What are you talking about, Dad?"

I said, "Well, all we do is ride motorbikes, play football, basketball, and all these physical things."

"Yeah?" he said, as if it didn't sound so bad. Frankly, it didn't sound so bad to me either.

"Well, your teacher seems to think you need some art and music and things like that in your life."

He looked past me and squinted, then looked into my eyes. "Dad, you gotta be kidding me."

I thought, *Well, so much for that. I said my piece and got it off my conscience.* If he'd said, "Yeah, let's go to the opera," I would have sent him off by himself. I wouldn't have been able to hack it myself.

To be honest, J.D. is a well-rounded collegian now, and he appreciates good music and art, though he's not deep in either area. I have no problem with intellectual pursuits, and I respect people who are gifted and interested in those areas. But I wouldn't force a kid into art or music if he would rather concentrate on sports any more than I would force a musician or an artist into football against his will. There are some people who are equally at home in either area, and that's great.

I wish I was more of a reader. I read slowly and have to really concentrate, and I know it drives my owner, Jack Kent Cooke, crazy. He's a voracious reader, and early in my career in Washington he used to recommend things for me to read. I finally told him, "Mr. Cooke, I'm really not much of a reader."

He winced and turned to his son and said, "Oh no, John, did you hear that? He's not a reader!" It pained him so much he'd probably rather have fired me for that than for any losing streak.

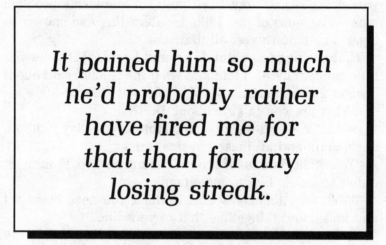

> *It pained him so much he'd probably rather have fired me for that than for any losing streak.*

Some of the times I've treasured most came when I was putting the boys to bed. It was Pat who got them up and rolling in the mornings and me who put them to bed. George Tharel always tried to sell me on having daily devotions, reading my Bible and commentary, which I try to do now. Back when the kids were growing up, I often shared things from the Bible with the boys before they went to sleep.

I cherished that time with the boys and always tried to find something good to share with them. I'd read and then we'd talk before they went to sleep. That was my time with them, and it was great for me. I hope it was for them. I always felt God honored that.

Kids are so precious when they're young. They're deadly honest. I remember telling Coy one Saturday night, "Now tomorrow we'll be back in God's house."

He goes, "Oh, no."

I say, "Why would you say that? On Sunday we want to be in the Lord's house."

He says, "I don't know why! He's never there. I've never seen Him."

That was funny, but it gave me the opportunity to talk about how God is with us, even when we can't see Him, and that He is in His house, especially when we worship Him.

A few years later Coy told me he wasn't sure he was going to like heaven.

"Why not?" I asked him.

"Because there's no risk. If I'm riding a bike or driving a car or riding a motorbike, I can't get hurt. What's the fun if there's no risk?"

What could I say? He was right! I wasn't sure I was going to like that part of it either. Part of the fun of life is the risk. We've both since learned that there will be plenty of good substitutes in heaven for the risk of injury. Forgive us, but as J.D.'s teacher so accurately pointed out, we're physical guys.

Decision, Decision

Don Coryell has been a huge influence in my coaching career. There's no question he is one of the greatest ever to have coached the game. *Sports Illustrated* rated him the third best coach ever. He won in high school, won in small college, won at San Diego State, won in pro ball. I found him a sincere guy who helped formulate a lot of my ideas about coaching football. He was progressive and liberal, which was great for me. As I've said, I tended to be rigid. He was the kind of a coach who let his assistants do their things. He let me assume a lot of responsibility and gave me room to succeed and fail.

For me, everything had to be perfect. For Don, looseness and flexibility were okay. Someone might want to change the snap count in the middle of the season. That would have made me angry. Don would say, "Fine, if it'll help, go ahead and do it." He was so good that way.

Before Don had come to St. Louis, it had been a long time since the Cardinals had won much. When he came, the climate was right. The personnel was in place, from the field to the front office. Though we started with a losing season, everything turned around the next year and we began to roll. We won the division a few times, got into the play-offs a couple of times. We were knocking at the door, a comer, a contending team that was fun to watch.

During my fifth season there, in 1977, we were playing a

big game against Washington at home. If we beat them, we'd be in the play-offs. But we lost. Don had been uptight because it seemed he hadn't been getting the players he wanted the last couple of seasons. So there was tension to begin with. Couple that with the loss and add that his wife had been sitting in the stands and had taken some abuse from some not-so-well-meaning fans, and you have the makings for a blowup. Don blew up.

When he got the chance at a press conference, he unloaded on management, the town, the fans, everyone. He's the kind of a guy who holds things inside until he's had enough, and anyone who has seen a loved one take heat knows that that is usually enough.

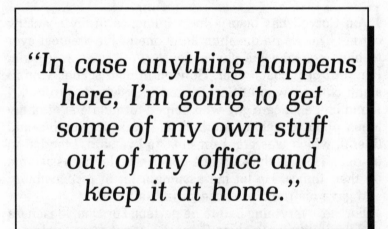

"In case anything happens here, I'm going to get some of my own stuff out of my office and keep it at home."

We coaches went back to work the following Monday as if nothing had happened, but the bad blood appeared in the papers and was on the talk shows all week. I started to get a feeling of doom, and I told Pat the next Saturday, "In case anything happens here, I'm going to get some of my own stuff out of my office and keep it at home."

I was a day late. My key had worked on Friday. On Saturday the lock wouldn't budge. I called Pat from a phone booth. "Why don't you look around the country and see if there's some other place you'd like me to coach. I think it's over."

Coryell and the owner had a parting of the ways, and the rest of the coaching staff was given permission to talk to other teams. When I got a call from my old friend John McKay, by then head coach of the Tampa Bay Buccaneers, I was ready. He wanted an offensive coordinator, and that was exactly what I wanted. I was coming up on thirty-eight years old. It was time to jump start this career.

Meanwhile, Pat's counsel against the racquetball club investment was proving right. The buildings were draining everyone involved. With several of us moving, that meant absentee ownership, and eventually we had to buy our way out of a worsening situation. The tab was well over a hundred thousand dollars, besides what we had already sunk into it. That should have been a lesson for me.

I hadn't yet learned that it was crucial to be in agreement with your wife on such a decision, and I didn't know how accurate her intuition could be. She never said "I told you so," or berated me, but she sure could have. I had virtually talked her into that deal, and I had been flat wrong. You'd think I would pledge never to get into another deal that didn't sound right to Pat. You'd be wrong.

That mess made my quest for a head coaching job even more important. I had two growing boys and a wife to provide for. I wanted to accumulate enough cash so I could take care of any one of them if anything ever happened. And I wanted them to be taken care of if anything happened to me. I would be making decent money now as Tampa Bay's offensive coordinator, but my investment debt and my growing family made that pretty thin. At my age I desperately needed another winning situation where I could be seen as a major part of the reason.

One of the first things I was asked to do in Tampa Bay was to check out a black quarterback named Doug Williams, a potential draft choice. There was little question of his fitness, his arm, his savvy, his physical ability. We wanted to know about his character and intelligence, vital issues for any NFL quarterback. I spent a lot of time with him, even saw him with children in a student teaching situation. I liked him and believed in him, and John Mc-

Kay had the guts to make him the first ever black quarter-back taken in the first round. He was signed, and he started off brilliantly for us. Everywhere I'd been on staff, we had been winners. This kid was going to help us do it again.

Then we played a couple of tougher teams, got some bad breaks and lost a few games. No problem. By mid-season we were still surprising people. Then Williams got his jaw broken. He was out. And the season fell apart. We lost almost all the rest of our games. I was in the pits.

Week after week as our record worsened and tempers grew short, we saw guys pointing the finger at one an-other, at the coaches, at management. No matter what we tried, nothing worked. The fans had no patience. I couldn't figure it out. How could this happen to someone who was committed to the Lord? I really *was* committed. I knew I had a long way to go, but I had trusted Him. I believed He led me to Tampa Bay. But for this? To be humiliated? To fail in my first year as an offensive coordinator? What would this do to my career? Why was it happening to me?

The season seemed longer and longer. We began to dread games rather than look forward to them. I sensed that my stock was falling. If I remained with the club I wondered if I would even stay in the same role. Would I still be calling plays, devising offensive strategy?

It wasn't fun anymore. It never is when you're losing, but I had not endured that before. This new experience was the worst. It was the first time I was facing major trauma in my life, and I began to question God. I didn't know where to turn. Losing a job, seeing an investment fall apart, those were nothing compared to this. I felt as if I was in the center of failure. I was in a place to make a difference, and even though I knew the odds were stacked against us, I felt personally responsible.

When the season was over I heard that Don Coryell had taken the San Diego Charger head coaching job. I prayed earnestly, "Do not have him call me, Lord, unless you want me to go with him." I meant it. I didn't want the ordeal of parting with John McKay or of moving my family across the country yet again unless it was what God wanted for me.

The next day, Coryell called. Now I had prayed in faith, believing that God would not let him call me unless a move was in God's will. I should have been at peace and excited.

"What would you want me to do, Don?"

"I want you to coach the offensive backfield."

My heart sank. "You don't need an offensive coordinator?"

"Got one. Ray Perkins is handling that for me."

"Oh." That meant I would be going back from being offensive coordinator at one place to backfield coach at another. My ego was in a quagmire. I had prayed, and that prayer had apparently been answered, but I was in the way of having peace about it. I was really torn. Should I stay or should I go?

I was in such a state that I could hardly concentrate or sleep. It was all I thought about. Should I go back and play for Don again but virtually take a step back in my search for a head coaching job? I wanted desperately to make an intelligent, correct, and spiritual decision. I conferred with everyone I trusted. I talked to Pat. I talked to my pastor. And I talked to George Tharel. None could or would make the decision for me, but I knew there was wisdom in talking with at least three people who were walking with the Lord.

I prayed and read a lot of Scripture, finally claiming several verses. James 1:2–6 says, "Count it all joy when you fall into various trials, knowing that the testing of your faith produces patience. But let patience have its perfect work, that you may be perfect and complete, lacking nothing. If any of you lacks wisdom, let him ask of God, who gives to all liberally and without reproach, and it will be given to him. But let him ask in faith, with no doubting, for he who doubts is like a wave of the sea driven and tossed by the wind."

Boy, that sure described me. I was doubting, wondering, questioning, and I felt as if I was being driven and tossed by the wind. The worst part was, I had got what I asked for. Why I couldn't see—except with hindsight—that God was leading me, I'll never know. I guess that's how He keeps us humble. The answer is before our eyes, and even after getting counsel from trusted people, we don't see it.

Things had been so frustrating at Tampa Bay that I sensed Coach McKay wanted to get back into calling the offensive plays himself. That would have been his right, of course, but where would that leave me? If I stayed just to keep the title of offensive coordinator, it wouldn't be right. I likely would not be doing that job the way it's supposed to be done. That, along with the fact that I had prayed about Coryell's call, should have given me plenty of direction. But I felt like I was in the wilderness. Shouldn't I rather have been a real offensive backfield coach than a pretend offensive coordinator? Clearly, I was thinking only of my résumé, my career, my future, when I should have left all of that with God.

One evening I met with Coach McKay to let him know what I was thinking. He deserved at least that. I was upfront and told him of the San Diego offer, my dilemma, everything. He's always been easy to talk to, a good and helpful guy. That night was no exception. He heard me out and was encouraging. Best of all (for my self-esteem), he was complimentary and wanted me to stay. That was the worst thing for my decision. Now I knew for sure he was behind me and wanted me, so if I decided to leave, it would be that much more awkward.

"I think you ought to stay," he said. Which was nice. I appreciated his being so positive, but I made no commitment. We left it that we would talk again the next day.

That night I tossed and turned. Unable to sleep, I prayed for long periods. Not only could I not make a decision, but I also didn't know *how* to make it. I was wasted by morning, and as I got ready to go see Coach McKay, Pat had some advice. By then I should have known that good counsel was one of the reasons God had put her in my life.

"Why don't you just let Coach McKay do the talking," she said. "And go from what he says."

As I drove to the office I thought hard about that. At my desk it was still working on me. *He knows I'm coming,* I thought, *so I'm just going to go in there and sit, and I'm not going to say a word.*

"Lord," I prayed, "whatever Coach McKay says, I'm going to act on that and make my decision accordingly."

On my way to his office I resolved to sit in silence for fifteen minutes if I had to. I was not going to speak first. As soon as I sat down, Coach McKay pulled out his yellow pad. "Joe," he began, "I made some notes after we talked last night, and there are some things I think we should talk about."

He talked about the year the Bucs had had and some decisions he had made about the future. He said, as I had suspected, that he wanted to be more personally responsible for calling the plays. "I just want you to be fully aware of where I'm coming from and what kind of a setup I want to have here next season, so you can make an intelligent decision."

To me it was clear as a bell. I had prayed about Don Coryell's call, and he had called. My wife had counseled me to let Coach McKay do the talking, and he had said just what I needed to convince me I should go. I had put out a fleece twice, so now my decision should be easy.

"Coach, what I think I'm going to do is to go back out to San Diego."

He nodded. "Well, you know I don't want you to go, but I understand. I really would like to have you stay here, and I want you to know you could stay as long as you want. You'd always have a job here."

He wasn't trying to pressure me. He was being straightforward as always. I admired his mind and his wit. We'd had some great times together and would always be friends. But I had made my decision.

I'd really like to say that after that period of turmoil, I

was now at peace. I had gone about the decision-making process correctly, had seen God answer in two distinct ways, and should have learned. I know this makes me sound pretty wishy-washy for a guy who saw himself as a potential head coach, but as soon as I left that office and made my call to accept the job in San Diego, I entered a period of doubt. Real doubt.

I was as miserable as I had ever been. Several nights in a row I would wake up at three or four in the morning in agony. Am I doing the right thing? I was backing down the career ladder, and I had no peace about it whatever.

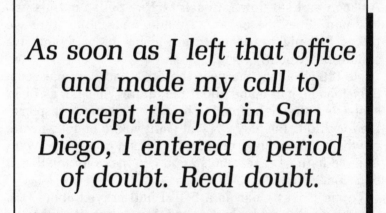

As soon as I left that office and made my call to accept the job in San Diego, I entered a period of doubt. Real doubt.

I read James 1 over and over and should have seen that I had gone about the decision the right way. But all I felt was confusion. I went to a man in our church whom I respected. He was a Bible teacher I knew to be close to God. "Can I ask you a question?" I said. "If a Christian makes a decision in what he felt was the right way, yet after he made it he thinks it was wrong, can God straighten it out? I mean, can He make the wrong decision work out right?"

He smiled and clicked his fingers, indicating that yes, God will honor a decision attempted correctly, even if it was wrong.

My problem was, I still didn't know if the decision was

right or wrong. All I knew was, I didn't feel good about
myself. I had made my decision, and I didn't feel any better than I would have if I had decided the opposite.

I couldn't go on like that. Before I moved to California,
Don Coryell asked me to work out some Charger draft
prospects in my area. Fortunately that work took me
within a few hundred miles of Arkansas. I could make up
my mind about one thing. I needed to see George Tharel.

Angel in the Night

Fayetteville was on the way to where I was going, so I boarded a plane, eager to see George. For days I had been in turmoil, questioning, doubting God, my faith in shambles. I prayed that George would put me on the right track as he had done so many times before. He had the wisdom, the right word, a letter just when I needed it.

As we flew into the northwest corner of Arkansas and settled into a holding pattern over Fayetteville, it became clear something was wrong. The engines droned endlessly as we sat above a snowstorm. Finally the captain announced that the landing had to be diverted.

I'm not terribly comfortable on airplanes anyway. It was stuffy, and I was sweating. And now I was mad. The plane was going to land in Fort Smith, about fifty miles south of Fayetteville on the Oklahoma–Arkansas border. It reminded me of when I heard about Coy's birth on the phone. Same deal. A plane in the snow, diverted from Fayetteville to Fort Smith.

The weather wasn't much better in Fort Smith, but they got the plane down. The weather was quickly upon us. A few planes were landing and a few were taking off toward the south. I was dumbfounded. How could God explain this? What did he want me to do? I was doing the best thing I knew. I was trying to see my spiritual counselor, trying to do the will of God, trying to seek His face. It

81

never dawned on me that He had already made it plain as day to me, that He had fulfilled my fleece and honored my requests.

My prayers just then were more challenges than entreaties. "God," I was saying, "what in the world are You doing to me?" Oh, I was really being a spiritual giant.

I had my hang-up bag and my heavy briefcase and was stomping from the plane to the terminal in the blowing snow when I overheard a couple of businessmen say something about renting a car and driving to Fayetteville. Perfect!

"You guys driving to Fayetteville now?"

They looked at me quizzically. "Yeah. Why?"

"I'm going with you."

I didn't ask them; I told them. Here I was, a husky guy in a suit and light overcoat, looking like I wanted to slug anybody who got in my way. They shrugged and I followed them to the car. I wasn't in the mood for chatter, but I overheard enough to know they were from Georgia. *Great!* I thought. *They've probably never driven in snow.*

They tried to ignore me as I threw my stuff in the back seat and got in. How could God be putting me through all this just to get to see George? It didn't make sense!

We were a few miles out of Fort Smith when the snow made it almost impossible to see. The pavement was ice glazed and a light layer of snow covered that. The driver was all over the road, and I could just see us winding up in a ditch or worse. In the middle of nowhere I said, "Pull over. I want to get out."

I heard one of the guys mutter, "Gladly, pal."

There was very little traffic from either direction, and now all I wanted to do was get back to Fort Smith and find a plane to Tampa. I had to crawl over the center divider of the freeway, bags and all, and I was in a rage. My glasses were fogged up and I was covered with snow as I shivered in the darkness, hoping drivers could see my thumb and not slide into me.

"God, why? Why won't You let me get to George? This is ridiculous! I'm sure You want me to talk to him!"

I finally hitched a ride back to the airport in Fort Smith and trudged to the counter. "You got any flights to Tampa yet tonight?"

> *My glasses were fogged up and I was covered with snow as I shivered in the darkness, hoping drivers could see my thumb and not slide into me.*

"One boarding in twenty minutes, sir."

I slapped my credit card on the counter, stuffed the ticket and boarding pass into my pocket, and lugged my stuff to a chair. I was so furious I could hardly see straight, but my anger was slowly turning to self-pity. I thought I had had the right idea. I thought my motive was right. I was trying to do the right thing. Failure had been a stranger until the racquetball club fiasco and the previous football season. Now I couldn't seem to succeed even in getting to see my old friend.

As I sat there feeling sorry for myself, I noticed a Bible. Now what would a Gideon Bible be doing in an airport? I wondered if it had been stolen from a hotel room. Maybe the Gideons put their Bibles everywhere in Arkansas. I picked it up and turned to James 1. I had claimed those verses, but so far I couldn't see how they applied. I read them again carefully. Where was God? What did He want from me in all of this? I believed He cared for me, but in my ignorance I thought I hadn't heard from Him at all.

As I read the passage in James, I sensed someone sitting next to me. I kept my eyes on the page. The man leaned over and looked at what I was reading. I didn't move. He tapped me on the shoulder and I looked up at a man about my age.

"I claimed that chapter in my life about six months ago," he said.

I was so taken aback by his sitting next to me, looking over my shoulder, and tapping me that I could hardly speak. "What?" I said, utterly confused. I wouldn't have been more puzzled if he said he was from outer space.

"Yeah," he said. "I claimed that chapter in my life. Let me tell you what happened."

I had said nothing but, "What?" and he volunteered his story. He spoke quickly, nonstop until it was time for me to board my plane.

"I was a pharmacist in Texas," he began, "and my job was the most important thing in life to me. I'd studied and prepared my whole life to get that job, and I loved it. Then I got the chance to move to Oklahoma and take over a bigger pharmacy. It would be a big promotion, a tremendous advancement for me. I believed it was of the Lord, so I quit my job in Texas and took it.

"Once I got there my new employers and I realized that I would have to be certified in Oklahoma, re-qualified by taking their state pharmaceutical test."

He told me in great detail about the test, how unbelievably demanding and technical and detailed it was. "There was no way," he said. "I had been out of school a long time. I didn't have the time to study for it, and I knew I wouldn't be able to pass. I would lose my job in Oklahoma and have to start over in Texas at a smaller place."

He tried to find some way around the requirement, but there was none. The bottom line was, "I had to try. I had made this gigantic career move, and it was going to be taken from me."

He said he prayed and read Scripture. "I was so uptight and distraught that I could hardly concentrate. I was driving myself crazy worrying about it, making my chances of passing even worse. Eventually I found peace about it. I said, 'God, you know what I want to do. I'm going to turn this back over to You and leave it in Your hands. All I can do is the best I can do."

He had claimed James 1 and rested in that. He would accept whatever outcome God had for him. "I studied as much as I could in the short time I had, went in and took the test, and did the best I knew how. You know what happened?"

I shook my head. I couldn't speak. I was still blown away by this stranger telling me this story in the middle of nowhere.

"I passed with a score in the nineties. It was unbelievable. A miracle. It couldn't have, shouldn't have happened. The bottom line conclusion I came to was that that job had the wrong priority in my life. It had become the most important thing to me. When I finally relaxed and turned it back over to the Lord, He put it in its proper place and gave it back to me."

I was stunned. He told me all that without my saying a word, let alone telling anything about my job, my situation, my doubts and fears. My flight was being announced. I stood and thanked him. I didn't even have time to tell him what his story meant to me. I walked to that plane as if in a trance. When I was settled in and had my bags stored and my coat off, I was able to relax. The fatigue of several days of lost sleep caught up with me. I was drowsy. I was no longer tense. I was going to be able to sleep.

I've been an idiot, I thought.

"Lord," I prayed, "thank you for putting that guy there and getting me there to hear what he had to say."

I had been trying to manage my career on my own. Much as I tried to tell myself otherwise, I was still on the throne. My path toward a head coach's job had consumed me. It clouded every decision, affected every choice. I'd applied to colleges. Only Missouri and Arizona would even interview me. I knew now that nothing like that had panned out because I wasn't ready, and God knew that.

"You know I still want to be a head coach," I prayed silently on that plane. "But maybe You don't want that for me—now or ever. I'm going to turn it over to You and quit worrying about it. No more fighting and striving and trying to do it myself. I'm going to relax and leave it in Your hands."

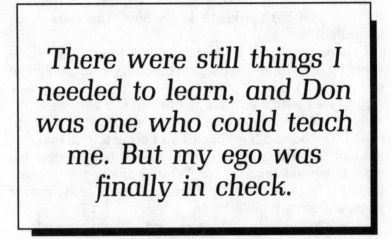

There were still things I needed to learn, and Don was one who could teach me. But my ego was finally in check.

Once I had prayed that prayer and entrusted God with my life's goal, my attitude changed. I dozed on the plane, was happy to get home, could relax, and was able to sleep soundly. I wanted to get to San Diego and serve under Don Coryell again and make the most of it. There were still things I needed to learn, and Don was one who could teach me. But my ego was finally in check. I was still going to be a working, get-after-it kind of a football coach, but there would be no more of this trying to determine my own future.

A week later I got to San Diego and started working with Don and the rest of the staff. Two days after that Don called me in. "Joe," he said, "are you still interested in the offensive coordinator job?" I couldn't speak. He knew the answer anyway.

"Perkins is leaving to be head coach of the Giants. You're my new offensive coordinator if you want it."

If I wanted it? I couldn't know then the success we'd

have, or that within two years I would be named head coach of the Redskins. All I knew was that the old adage was again proved true: God reserves His very best for those who leave the timing to Him.

You could look at all that and say I had a series of lucky breaks, but I don't think so. Nobody could take that many career steps over that many years and have it turn out so perfectly, unless God was in it. As I look back, I see His hand all along the way, when I was away from Him and when I was close, when I was trusting and when I was doubting. He guided me to where I am today, but I had to get out of His way to let it happen.

To try to explain some other way that snowstorm in Fayetteville, that rerouting to Fort Smith, that hitchhiking back, that Bible in the airport, that stranger with a story just for me—that would be futile. My life view, my world view, won't allow it. To believe that was all coincidence and happenstance would be like saying that this world and all our loved ones are here by accident, by chance, by two amoebas bumping together in a cosmic pool in eternity past. It doesn't wash.

I could either say these things just happened and events in our lives simply fall one way or the other as they will, or I can say, hey, Somebody made me, Somebody loves me, Somebody is directing my life and will continue if I dedicate it to Him. He is all-knowing. He never sleeps. His eyes roam to and fro across the earth, and He cares about me. As long as I stay in fellowship with Him and maintain my relationship with Him, that's all I care about. He will take care of the rest.

What a comfort it was to put even my success and happiness in His care. If neither was what He had in mind for me, I would be content with that too. What I didn't know fully yet was that pain and trials are just as much a part of the journey.

Pat

You don't hear too much about football coaches' wives for some reason. By necessity they are stay-at-home, behind-the-scenes types. Right or wrong, football is a man's game. Think of all the post-game celebrations you've seen. You hardly see any women on the field. The wives are in the stands or in a box or at home watching on TV.

They're involved, make no mistake about that. Football wives quickly learn the game and the nuances, and for the most part they know what's going on. They know what worked and they know what didn't work. They know when their husbands have succeeded and when they have screwed up.

I've always felt bad that Pat was in the background in my career. No, I wouldn't want her charging onto the field, even after a Super Bowl win, because I would be afraid for her safety. That's one of the things I hate about what I do. Pat seems to be on the outside until I hook up with her in the car after the game. She's not really there, right with me, in person, to experience the highs and lows. Her connection is sort of second hand. It takes a special woman to be a football coach's wife. If she's not a good wife, first of all, she'll never adjust to the life-style. And if that happens, the coach becomes ineffective too. There aren't many head coaches with bad marriages because a distracted coach is a bad coach and won't last long.

Pat is perfect for me and always has been. During our long courtship after meeting in high school, we had our ups and downs and our fights. But we always knew we would wind up married, best friends, and partners for life. She has a great sense of humor and gift of gab. We enjoy each other and we enjoy life. I can't imagine life without her.

She can certainly imagine life without me, because half the year or so, I'm not around much. I told myself that she hated that, and I felt guilty about it for years. When I talk to her and the boys about it in the off-season, though, they say they have accepted my absence as one of the givens of my profession. There are many advantages, too, in having a husband and father who is a pro coach, so I guess they figure it's a trade off.

Frankly, I have discovered that the family has learned to get along without me just fine. In fact, I get the distinct impression that when I do rejoin them each year during the off-season, I'm basically an obstacle to the routine they're used to. I might try to make decisions on something that's already family policy. I might try to upset the schedule with my impromptu ideas and get everyone to run out with me for a sandwich or a swim or whatever. They roll their eyes and inform me that they have schedules and responsibilities. They are not as free as I am to do what I want when I want to.

I get finished with the football season and look forward to that freedom, but then I find myself in the middle of a homestead where another system, every bit as regimented, is already in place. If forced, my wife would probably admit that she's used to my being gone and that when it gets near football season, she starts to look forward to it. Poor me.

Pat doesn't like it, when she has to get hold of me during training camp or during the season and I'm impossible to reach. Sometimes I forget to remind everybody that my do-not-disturb instruction does not include my own wife, and someone will tell her, "He's sleeping" or "He's unavailable" or "He's in a meeting" or "He can't be disturbed." She knows I'm busy, and she wouldn't have called if she could have avoided it. So when she doesn't get through, I always hear about it, and rightly so.

In the eyes of the world, she's in the background. Her work is not as visible, and thus, to some people, not as important. But my work would be nothing without a wife like her. What most people don't realize is that something is as true in my family as it is in almost any man's family: What our wives do and have done is much more valuable in terms of eternity than anything we could ever do. Ten years from now my name may appear in the Redskin Hall of Fame because my teams have won a lot of football games. That will be my legacy. By then I will be a fan, going to games and cheering along with everyone else. I have no illusions about that.

> *Her work is not as visible, and thus, to some people, not as important. But my work would be nothing without a wife like her.*

But Pat's accomplishments, unknown to most people, will be honored for eternity. She has been father and mother to our boys while I spent months leaving the house early and getting home late, investing my time in a game.

I don't want to be too hard on myself. I worked at raising my kids and trying to impart spiritual truth. I once told one of my kids that George Tharel was my spiritual father, and he asked Pat if his own father could also be his spiritual father. That meant a lot to me. I would love to be viewed that way by my sons. They will be my true legacy. I want what I do to count for eternity too, and sometimes the only way to do that is to share my faith with other people when I get a chance to speak. But my point here is to turn the spotlight on Pat for a minute, because even if no one this side of heaven is aware of her real value, I am.

I once heard a man begin to speak about his wife, then catch himself. "I don't have enough time to tell you everything about her," he said, "but you can read about her in Proverbs 31."

I'm not saying Pat and I always see eye to eye. In fact, maybe because we don't, my profession is just right. Maybe she sees all of me she can stand each year. She's become self-reliant and a take-charge type of a woman. She's had to. It takes a while each year for her and the boys to adjust to the old boss coming back into the picture. She says, "Now we have to eat what you want to eat, park where you want to park, and I'm not the head of the household."

She laughs about the annual dinner for the coaches and their wives before the team goes off to training camp. "The men are apologetic," she says. " 'Sorry we have to leave you wives all alone with the kids.' What they don't know is that most of us are saying, 'Oh good, they're gone to training camp for six weeks.' "

We do have a lot of fun together, but usually it's with other couples. Oh, we try. We go off together alone for a vacation, and the first day will be great. We'll relax, get a massage, sit by the pool. The second day I start looking around for something to do. Pat is enjoying the sun. I'm looking for a place to run or play. By the third day I'm going berserk trying to scrounge up a game of racquetball or something. By the fourth day we're bickering and admitting that we'd better invite someone to join us so we can have a good time.

Mostly, though, we're a good match. We see a lot of things alike. Our tastes and goals are the same. We don't consider ourselves intellectuals, but we like to discuss things. In other ways, we are opposites. There are times when if I would say white, she would say black. If I want to do this, she wants to do that. Of course, I need a wife who will stand up for her own opinions. She doesn't let me get complacent or uppity.

I could come a few days before the Super Bowl and be thinking I'm pretty special. At work, what I say goes. If people disagree with me there, they do it respectfully. But at home I'm just the dad. I leave something in the middle of the floor and I'm likely to hear, "Hey, Super Bowl coach, pick up your socks!"

During the middle of our years in St. Louis, in 1975, Pat began to detect some hearing loss in her left ear. There was no pain, but the loss was acute enough that she went to a doctor. He checked her thoroughly and suggested that sometimes a tumor, called an acoustic neuroma, can cause hearing loss. But no tumor was detected. The doctor concluded that a complication from one of Pat's pregnancies could have caused it, or she might have even suffered damage from a loud noise.

Pat didn't make a big deal of it, so I didn't either. I felt badly for her, but since she seemed to be coping with it, I was simply proud of her. She favored her right ear, but the loss of hearing in one was something we felt we could live with.

Eventually she grew completely deaf in the left ear. By the time we were in San Diego five years later, she noticed other symptoms—of what she didn't know. There was numbness in her left cheek and an irritation of her left eye. Without telling me, she went to an eye doctor who told her that her tear duct was not functioning. He prescribed an ointment, and when Pat began to also experience headaches, he suggested that she see an ear specialist again too.

The ear man put together the numbness, the tear duct problem, the hearing loss, and the headaches and immediately ordered a CAT scan. Why didn't Pat tell me? I was being touted as the pilot of Air Coryell. The Chargers were winning. The offense was breaking records. We were on our way to a division championship behind the passing of Dan Fouts to three all-pro receivers. Pat didn't want to bother me. There's a football wife for you. When the CAT scan in late November of 1979 revealed an acoustic neuroma that had been growing for about five years, Pat was worried less about that than about having her head shaved for surgery. Though her doctor was fairly confident the growth was noncancerous, it still had to be removed before it caused more severe damage. And still, she didn't tell me.

One night in December I arrived home and knew something was wrong. Pat was quiet, and it was clear she had been crying. I got her to tell me that she had been having more problems with the left side—her ear, her eye, her cheek, headaches, and that she had been to see the doctors. The upshot was that she had been optimistic. I say she was running from it. She says she just wanted to believe the best and not do anything before the end of the season. But that day her doctor had called and said it was "major, major." He recommended a specialist in Los Angeles and urged her to see him immediately.

"Well," I said, "that's what you're going to do then."

"Joe, the season isn't over. You can't go."

"Of course I can."

"No, now I'll go if you promise not to. I'll find out what he says and tell you everything."

Like a dummy, I agreed. I thought she'd heard the worst of it, that there was a tumor that had to be removed. It was noncancerous but serious. What more could the specialist have to say?

Plenty.

A guy who has done hundreds of similar operations has learned to cut through the denial and the fear and may be a little less sensitive than a first-time patient requires. Here was Pat, in L.A. while I'm in San Diego, sitting in the office of a doctor who didn't mean to be ruthless, but who was telling it like it was.

"I'd like you to sign this release," he said, sliding it across the desk. "It states that you understand the risks with this kind of surgery. You could have paralysis on the left side of your face if there is nerve damage. Your eyelid could remain predominantly open. . . ." He went on and on with all the potential complications.

Pat was good at cutting through the bull too. "I'll sign this," she said, not admitting she was devastated at all the possibilities, "but just give me the bottom line. How many have you lost."

"Well, in twenty years of this type of surgery, we have lost one patient."

"And what was the reason?"

"Hemorrhaging following surgery."

Pat liked the odds, but she was in a shambles over all the maladies listed on the release form. What was going to happen to her? What would she look like? I'll probably never get over wishing I'd been there with her for that meeting. I had no idea. From that time on, we were in that thing together.

Pat has always been a striking woman. She's beautifully dark with large, perfectly symmetrical features. Her smile lights up a room. I cherished that about her, but I was not in love with her looks. I was in love with her, her person, her character, her spirit. I loved the person she was, not just the body in which she resided.

The doctor told us that the tumor was growing slowly enough that a few more weeks wouldn't make much difference. She would not be in any more critical danger after Christmas than she was right then, so we agreed on January 2, 1980, for her surgery in Los Angeles.

Over the next few weeks I concentrated on finishing up the season with the Chargers and keeping Pat's spirits up. She was still looking on the bright side, as I was, but there was no question we were both shook up and scared. Our boys were almost eleven and seven. We didn't want to think of their losing their mother or having her handicapped.

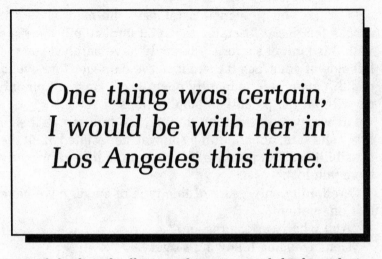

*One thing was certain,
I would be with her in
Los Angeles this time.*

We did a lot of talking and praying and thinking during that time. One thing was certain, I would be with her in Los Angeles this time. Nothing could keep me from that.

Surgery

The specialist and the neurosurgeon carefully explained the procedure. The operation would not be simple but shouldn't be too long either, three to four hours. They would make an incision behind Pat's ear and drill a hole through the skull into the acoustic canal. The specialist had custom designed instruments that allowed access to the tumor through there. It would be carefully removed, the swelling and bleeding monitored, and then she would be sewn back together and wheeled to the recovery room. Shortly after she came to, I would be allowed to see her, though she would be groggy.

I was more encouraged than I had been since Pat first told me about it. The doctors were still a bit cold and direct, and while I felt for Pat having to hear all that, I wanted to know everything. I was glad they told me the truth. They sure seemed to know what they were doing, and I figured it was going to be pretty much straightforward. It was serious, but it was a procedure the specialist had done hundreds of times with an almost perfect rate of success. Now *I* was the optimistic one.

I was still nervous as I paced the halls, praying for Pat and thinking of the great life we had together with the boys. I didn't want anything to jeopardize that, even though I knew she would need a long time to get back to

101

full strength and speed. Yet I was hopeful. We'd been through crises before. We would come through this.

Near the four-hour mark I was getting antsy. Loved ones of surgical patients have a sixth sense about this, and I knew that in a few more minutes it would be time to be concerned, if not downright worried.

Just then I saw the specialist and the neurosurgeon come briskly down the hall with huge grins. "It went great," they said. "Just great."

I couldn't keep from smiling. I shook their hands, congratulated them, and thanked them.

"She's in recovery right now," the specialist said. "I'll have them call you as soon as you can see her. It should be just a few minutes." I breathed a silent prayer. When a specialist like that seems elated after surgery, I have to be thrilled. Now I could go sit somewhere and relax. I didn't feel like pacing anymore. I couldn't wait to see Pat, even though she would probably be too out of it to recognize me. I figured I'd see lots of swelling and maybe discoloration, but I was prepared for that.

I sat and flipped through a magazine, but I wasn't ready to read just yet. I tried to will the time to pass. The clock moved slowly. Somehow I was able to distract myself and calm down. Soon I realized that forty-five minutes had gone by. I hurried down the hall to the nurses' station.

"Hey, listen, you know anything about Mrs. Gibbs? She's supposed to be in the recovery room and I was supposed to—"

"Sir," the nurse said. "I believe there's a call for you in the waiting room."

I jogged back and picked up the ringing phone. It was the neurosurgeon. "Mr. Gibbs, we're taking your wife back into surgery. We think we have bleeding in there. I'll call you when we're through."

"Wait a minute," I said. "Let me talk to the specialist."

"He's already left, sir."

> ## "Mr. Gibbs, we're taking your wife back into surgery. We think we have bleeding in there. I'll call you when we're through."

"Well, is there a phone in the operating room?"

"No, sir. I mean he's left the hospital."

"What?!"

"We just now discovered this complication, sir, and he had already left. I'll call you."

They had warned Pat of this. Hemorrhaging was what cost such patients their lives. When a tumor that old and large (golf ball size) has been putting pressure on the brain for so long, removing it causes problems. With the tumor gone, the brain is free to settle back down into the cranial cavity. Not used to being there, the blood vessels that have atrophied can stretch until they rupture. That causes the bleeding.

I slumped into a chair feeling as alone as I had ever felt. For the first time I had a real fear that I would lose Pat. I prayed that God would spare her. The only patient they had ever lost had hemorrhaged after surgery and they had not gotten back in in time to fix the problem. I could only hope and pray they had discovered Pat's bleeding early enough. If she survived, what damage would the hemorrhaging cause?

I found a nurse in the recovery area and asked her how they knew to take Pat back into surgery. "Your wife passed out, sir," she said. "She had come around a little after the operation and we were about to ask you to come and see her. When she seemed to get drowsy again, we knew it couldn't be the anesthesia. When she lost consciousness, the neurosurgeon examined her and got her into the operating room right away."

"So you caught it pretty quickly."

"Well, we hope so. She was back in there just minutes after she passed out. Now she has to be anesthetized again, which is always risky, but he should be able to control the bleeding—if that's the problem—by cauterizing the faulty blood vessels and using an anti-inflammatory agent."

"If that's the problem? It could be something else?"

"They never know until they check. An X-ray or CAT scan would take too long, and since she had just come from surgery . . . "

"Uh-huh."

I went back to the waiting room to pray. I pleaded with God. How would I tell J.D. and Coy and our relatives? What would I do without her? As I prayed I sensed that God was with me, that He heard me, and that He had answered me. At first I didn't know if the answer was that He would be with me whether she survived or not, or if He had protected her from death. Within a few minutes I believed she was going to make it. I wasn't sure why. I just felt it.

Over the next hour and a half my faith wavered and strengthened, wavered and strengthened. If it was just a bleeding problem and the surgeon could anesthetize her and go right back in, why should it take so long? Maybe that wasn't the problem. Maybe it was something even more serious. Maybe they had already lost her and were trying to revive her. Maybe the news would be the worst.

Then I would pray again and regain confidence. I couldn't shake the feeling that God would spare her. Talk about wanting something. I would have done anything to keep Pat alive. The worst part for an action-oriented person was to know that there was nothing I could do.

Finally the word came. I jumped out of that chair. She

was in intensive care and I could see her. I'll never forget how informal and almost haphazard it was in there, especially for an ICU. A bunch of people huddled around her, working on her, waking her up every fifteen minutes, and trying to talk to her. She had tubes down her throat that made her thrash against them and try to pull them out. The attendants all spoke with accents, which I could see also bothered Pat. She's not prejudiced, but she was in pain and frightened, and she wanted people around her who could understand her and whom she could understand.

She looked good, considering what she had been through and was going through.

A young doctor stood nearby. I looked at him pleadingly, not having to put my question in words.

"She's going to be fine," he said. "We have her restrained so she can't pull the tubes out, because if she relapses we don't want to have to put them back in."

"How long does she have to have them in?"

"About three hours."

Choking and gagging, she banged the sides of the bed, but there was no budging from those leather wrist straps. I looked closely at her face for signs of paralysis. I thought she looked okay, but it was killing me to see her struggle and suffer.

The young doctor was about to move on. I stood at the foot of the bed and grabbed his arm. "You can't go," I said. "Please don't leave until she gets these things out of her mouth."

"I really need to check on some other—"

"Hey, listen, you're staying here with me until my wife gets those tubes out of her throat."

Those were the worst three hours of my life. I would rather have been in that situation myself than to see someone I loved endure it. Finally they felt confident enough to take the tubes out, and she was able to get some sleep. I went back to the waiting room and really relaxed for the first time in hours.

When I got to see Pat again, her left eye was taped shut. There were plans to do a routine follow-up procedure to put some sort of spring-loaded clip in her eyelid to allow the eye to shut when she relaxed. Of course, the "routine follow-up procedure" was another word for surgery. I had no idea she'd be in the operating room for another two hours, and I certainly had no idea she would look worse than she had the first time.

I didn't know it then, but Pat had already gotten a glimpse of her face. She wasn't supposed to see it, and though she was having trouble with the whole left side of her body, as if she'd had a stroke, she somehow maneuvered the bed tray to where she could pop up that little mirror in the middle. She didn't tell me then, but she was horrified. She knew what her face felt like—nothing—and now she knew what it looked like. Of course, the doctors had told us there would be temporary swelling and discoloration and even paralysis, but they also predicted that that would gradually clear up.

After the second operation four days later, I was furious. I had expected much worse the first time but had been pleasantly surprised. Now, I expected this "procedure" to be some small slit in the eyelid. She was swollen, black and blue, the left side of her face drooping from paralysis as if she'd been to a dentist from hell. I knew it was temporary but I was angry I had not been properly prepared for it.

The next day J.D. and Coy saw her. Maybe they shouldn't have. One has an aversion to hospitals to this day. When we were finally able to take her home after eight days in ICU and ten more in a regular ward, she needed a walker, she had trouble talking, and her left hand was weak. She still looked like a stroke victim. One of the boys doted on her, worried that she would fall over in public. The other pretended not to be with her. Both reactions were normal, we think.

Needless to say, I was not too happy that the specialist

had left the hospital when he thought everything was fine after the first surgery. At our final checkup with him, I told him straight out, "I don't think there would have been as much nerve damage if you'd have been here."

I expected him to say that his presence had nothing to do with it, but he said nothing. That was probably the safest thing legally. Of course we weren't going to sue, but I'm sure that crossed his mind. It could be, too, that he knew I was right. He should have stayed there until she was completely out of the woods. I'm sure the neurosurgeon did all he could, but he hadn't done hundreds of those operations either.

Pat says she tried not to think about how she looked. She has a way of shutting out negative thoughts, and I'm impressed with that. She knew I would never be embarrassed by her; she worried about what others would think and say. "I was embarrassed for you," she says.

Her recovery was long and slow. The clip in her eye never worked a hundred percent, so she still has to lubricate that eye. The paralysis in the left side of her face is not as bad as it was when she came out of the hospital, but it's still there. She has been incredibly good about it.

"I didn't like seeing a face in the mirror that didn't look like my face," she says. "I hated myself. I guess I was reacting like a burn victim. It was horrible, but Joe was so good. He never said, 'Oh, here we go again, crying about something you can't change.' He let me go through it. He let me grieve my loss. He never said, 'Oh, don't be silly.' I really appreciated that.

"At first I cried every day. Then I cried once a week. Then I cried once a month. I seldom cry about it anymore."

The change in her face is noticeable, and naturally she doesn't want people staring at her or feeling sorry for her. She has not let it slow her in the least. She approaches new acquaintances and jokes with them, in that way letting them know that she doesn't consider her new look a handicap and they shouldn't worry about it either. She's maintained her great sense of humor. Recently, when someone took a picture of her with the boys, one of them put his arm around her and playfully lifted her cheek for the photo.

Pat told me one time that she had questioned why this trauma had entered her life. She said it was possible that the farther I went in my career, the more proud she might have become. "Who knows?" she says. "As the wife of an NFL coach, I might have really become a snob."

She wouldn't have, and we discussed that only once, but it was interesting to me that she was looking for a reason. "I belong to God," she says. "And I believe he allows things to come into our lives for a reason. Just because I don't know the reason doesn't mean there isn't one. Maybe this has just made me more sensitive to other people with problems."

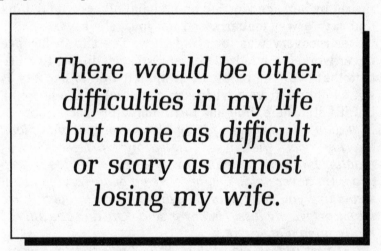

There would be other difficulties in my life but none as difficult or scary as almost losing my wife.

She's dealing with it. It's been more than ten years now and is part of our lives. I'm proud to introduce her anywhere. Surgery may have slightly altered her looks, but it did not change her character. She's still Pat.

I'll tell you, going through something like that with the person you love sure makes losing a football game seem trivial. I had asked God why He had let me endure that horrible season in Tampa, and why I had been so blind and faithless when I had no peace about His leading me to

San Diego. In a small way, I think, He was preparing me for this real trial.

There would be other difficulties in my life but none as difficult or scary as almost losing my wife. I still had a lot to learn about priorities and my faith and my ego, but I could never again say that God hadn't led me through some deep waters to strengthen me for when those new lessons came.

What a Start!

Almost exactly a year after Pat's surgery, I got the late night call from Bobby Beathard about the Washington job. After the intimidating but thrilling meeting with Jack Kent Cooke in New York, I admit I studied how new coaches had done over the years with the Redskins. I had to do something with those sleepless nights. What an unbelievable week! I had left the timing with God, and He had provided the job of my dreams. I became the seventeenth Washington head coach.

In studying Redskin history I learned that Ray Flaherty, the first coach, was 47–16–1 over six years (1937–42) for a .735 winning percentage and induction in the Pro Football Hall of Fame. That was a little formidable. The first ever Redskin team had won the world championship.

The guy I was replacing, Jack Pardee, had taken over after the legendary George Allen. Allen had amassed the most victories of any Washington coach, going 67–30–1 from 1971 to 1977 and never having a losing season. In fact, Allen had only two seasons in which he lost more than four games, and he had taken the Redskins to their only Super Bowl appearance (after the 1972 season; they lost 14–7 to the Dolphins).

Pardee had followed Allen by speeding off to a great start in 1978, winning his first six games, seven of his first nine, and eight of his first eleven, before seeing it all fall

113

apart. The Skins lost their last five games that season to wind up at 8–8.

The 1979 Skins won six of their first eight and finished 10–6. Pardee was named NFL Coach of the Year. The next year, however, they dropped five of their first six and had to win their last three to get to 6–10. Then it was my turn. The ownership, the fans, and the press wanted a turn-around. They wanted consistency, and they wanted it fast.

I was optimistic. I had been preparing for this all my life. I had ideas. I knew how to run an offense. I knew what I wanted to see on defense, in the training room, on the practice field. I had good rapport with my coaches, and they were the men I wanted. Our player personnel was better than average, and where we needed help, Bobby and the scouts were going after it.

One of the first things I heard when I got to Washington was that I really needed to re-sign the great running back, John Riggins. He had sat out a year in a salary dispute, and he was one guy who could turn a franchise around. Without saying anything to anybody, I got on a plane and flew to Lawrence, Kansas. I rented a car and drove to the first gas station I saw and asked a guy if he knew where John Riggins lived.

He directed me to a country road where I located his house. John's wife Mary Lou answered the door and told me John wasn't there. I knew right away I had a good shot, because it was clear to me that she was very interested in seeing John come back to play football. She promised to call me at my hotel when John returned. The next morning I had a message to call her. She said he was home and that I could come and have breakfast with them.

When I arrived John was wearing hunting fatigues and drinking a beer. I look at this guy and I'm thinking, *Goodness gracious, what in the world? This guy's off the deep end!*

At breakfast I made my pitch, telling him how important I thought it was that he come back. I told him that even if he didn't feel he could play for the Redskins, we'd work something out to get him traded. I said he should get back into football while he was still in his prime. Toward the end of the conversation—he hadn't said much—he looked over at me and said, "I'll tell you what. If you get me back, I'll make you famous."

> *"All right," he said, "I want to come back, but the only team I want to play for is the Washington Redskins."*

I thought, *This guy is crazy. He's an egomaniac and he's nuts!* In the car I realized that the first thing I had to do when I got back was to get him signed and trade him. Back in Washington I got a call a week later from John. "All right," he said, "I want to come back, but the only team I want to play for is the Washington Redskins."

You know what? We signed him. And he made me famous.

We hold six weeks of summer camp for the Redskins at Dickinson College in Carlisle, Pennsylvania, about midway between Philadelphia and Pittsburgh. One thing I wanted to do was to take J.D. and Coy with me. They were probably too young that first year, but I took the chance anyway. J.D. was twelve and Coy was eight and a half. They would stay with Bobby Beathard's boys and

Richie Petibon's boy, who was about sixteen, downstairs in the dorm.

As I helped them unload their stuff and decide who was going to sleep where, I realized that my kids were the youngest of the bunch and that Coy was the very youngest by several years. I wondered if I was doing the right thing. I would be as busy as I'd ever been, interacting with players, teaching, coaching, looking at film, meeting with my coaches every night. There was no way I could keep track of Coy. And he was too young to be on his own.

Sad to say, as soon as I got with the players and coaches, I didn't give the kids a second thought for a couple of days. I saw them from a distance in the cafeteria and running around the grounds. I knew the Beathard boys and young Richie Petibon were good kids. How much trouble could they get into?

The second day there, I turned to go upstairs and a chocolate ice cream cone whizzed past my ear and stuck to a window at the top of the stairs. I whirled around to see who threw it, and there were all the kids at the bottom, frozen in place, looking as innocent as they could. I looked back up and saw that their target had not been the window. It had been Coy.

He was already covered with chocolate. His face was a mess. I could see he hadn't slept more than a couple of hours since he'd been there. He had dark circles under his eyes and a vacant look.

"Who threw that cone?" I asked him.

He wouldn't say. I looked at the culprits, looking pure as choirboys now.

"You don't tell me and you're gonna clean that mess up by yourself."

Coy wouldn't tell me. He started cleaning the window.

"When you get done I want you to get a shower and get some sleep." He looked relieved, as if he never would have thought of that himself, but now that his dad was *making* him, he'd just have to do it. J.D. told me later that Coy had been eating junk for two days and had stayed up

most of the night with the guys, eating pizzas and spying
on a class of little ballerinas who were also on campus.

"If they ask him how old he is, he's going to say
twelve!" J.D. told me.

Coy slept almost twenty-four hours, and I felt guilty for
having turned him loose. But he was having the time of his
life. He probably thought it was the best thing that had
ever happened to him.

The next night I was walking across campus with a
couple of the coaches, including one of Coy's favorites,
Lavern Torgeson. No one knew that the boys were hiding
in the bushes, spying on and waiting to scare or impress
the ballerinas. No one knew, that is, until Coy couldn't
control himself.

"Hi, Coach Torgy!" he hollered, and the other boys
shushed him and dragged him back into the bushes. What
a big time operator, impressing the girls and hiding from
Dad! But he had to say hi to Torgy!

When the six-week camp was finally over, I went
downstairs to help the boys carry their stuff to the car.
The hall and the four rooms the boys had been in were a
mess. Shaving cream, water, and garbage were all over
the place. I was livid, and I went crazy. Here I am, the
new head coach, about to check out of camp, and here's a
mess that has to be cleaned up. I mean, the place was a
wreck.

I had to be beet red. "J.D.," I said, "I want to know who
did this."

He looked me right in the eye, knowing full well they
had all been in on it. "I don't know, Dad."

"Tell me, J.D. was it Beathard's boys? Was it Richie?
Who? I want to know."

"I don't know, Dad. But I'll clean it up."

"You bet your life you will," I said. It took two maids
and J.D. and me almost ninety minutes to get that place
looking half normal.

Later Richie Petibon told me that his son was impressed
and had said, "J.D. didn't rat, Dad. He went down with the
ship. He's okay."

In the 1981 pre-season we beat Kansas City 16–10, Minnesota 27–13, and Baltimore 13–7 before losing to New England 19–10. As we got ready for our September 6 home opener against the Dallas Cowboys, I believed we had the makings of a contender. We were going to play well and beat some good football teams. Had it been worth it to move my family from coast to coast? We'd soon find out. Bobby and Mr. Cooke had made a serious gamble on an untested and relatively unknown forty-year-old. One of my biggest goals was to prove worthy of their trust.

More than 55,000 jammed RFK Stadium on that cloudy, warm Sunday. By kickoff, the temperature had risen to nearly eighty. The first period was scoreless. Dallas took the lead early in the second quarter on a 33-yard pass from Danny White to Billy Joe DuPree, but five minutes later we matched them when Joe Theismann hit Joe Washington with a 15-yarder.

White hit Drew Pearson with a 42-yard TD pass three minutes later and the Cowboys took a 14–7 lead into halftime. Five field goals made up all the scoring in the second half, but four of those were by Dallas' Rafael Septien and only one by our Mark Moseley. We had lost, 26–10.

I felt good about our defense in the second half, especially against a team like Dallas, a perennial winner. The score looked bigger than it was, having been run up mostly by field goals. We had matched the Cowboys with twenty first downs, but their rushing game was clearly better. We gave up 244 yards on the ground alone, 132 to Tony Dorsett. Joe Washington led our receivers with 124 yards, and Theismann completed 22 passes for 281 yards, but we had netted only 44 rushing yards.

I was still optimistic looking toward the next Sunday, another home game before a packed house. The morning broke hot and cloudless, and by game time against the New York Giants, it was 85 degrees. Our defense was great again as we held the Giants scoreless in the first half. But we were having trouble getting untracked, and we didn't score until the third period ourselves. Theismann hit Ricky Thompson with a short pass, and we enjoyed our first lead of the new season, 7–0.

The rest of the game, however, belonged to the Giants. Two touchdowns and a field goal gave them the 17–7 win, and I still hadn't tasted that first victory. There wasn't much to be proud of in that one either. We made only ten first downs, and New York more than doubled our total net yards.

I wanted to be patient. I didn't want to panic. I had hoped to fit Redskin personnel into what had worked for us in San Diego. Then I realized that was a mistake. The pre-season had been great, but now nothing was working. I followed my hunches and started tinkering with the backfield. Somehow the offense had to gel before we would be more productive.

We continued tinkering with the offense, knowing we had the people to get the ball in the end zone. We made a philosophical change and returned to the idea of a one-back setup. We hoped it would make our offense take off. It did.

The next Sunday saw us at St. Louis where we dominated the Cardinals in almost every statistic except the important one: points. We had 24 first downs to their 18. We had 521 net yards to their 315. Theismann was 25 for 37 for 388 yards in the air, and two of our receivers, Thompson and Art Monk, caught more than 100 yards worth of passes each.

Time of possession was almost dead even. Late in the second quarter the game had still been close. We trailed just 19–17 after a 79-yard touchdown pass from Theismann to Monk. The next three TDs were the Cards', and by early in the final quarter we trailed 40–17. We finished with two TD passes in about five minutes but still lost 40–30.

Now it was getting frustrating. We felt we were getting on track, but still we had lost. We were playing tough, competitive football in the first half, then getting beaten up in the second half. I could have been encouraged by our offense late in that game, but when a team is leading 40–17, it has to let down a little. I'm sure they were even experimenting with some of their second stringers on defense.

We were 0–3. I kept telling myself there had to be a reason for this. I didn't want to—and never would—just sit back and accept losing, because I knew there was some cosmic purpose in it. I did believe that God has a reason for letting anyone go through adversity, but that sure didn't stop me from trying to put the brakes on it. I had an owner, a general manager, ten assistant coaches, a front office staff, a wife, and two kids who were suffering every bit as much as the players and I were suffering. That's one of the parts about being a head coach that I had not given much thought to. When I was an assistant I bled when we lost, but I didn't feel the weight of everyone else's pain. This was awful.

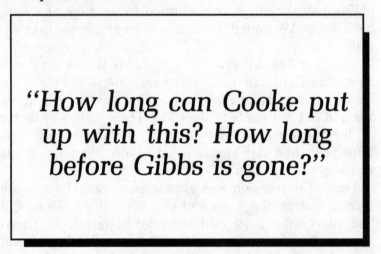

"How long can Cooke put up with this? How long before Gibbs is gone?"

The talk in the papers and on the talk shows and on the streets—where my family could hear it—was, "How long can Cooke put up with this? How long before Gibbs is gone?"

I was determined to continue working hard, looking for

character in players. Would they become finger pointers or would they hunker down and turn things around? Would they give up, slack off, stop working hard? I was getting to know my players in a way I might not have if they had been winning every week. The coaches and I were getting to know each other, the G.M. and I, the owner and I. If I had to choose whether I wanted an owner who was a rock during the bad times or a rock during the good times, I'd choose the first. I will never forget how good Mr. Cooke was during this time when the Redskins' record was an embarrassment to everyone.

Somehow we needed to strike early and stay strong on defense for four quarters. Our next test was at Philadelphia against the Eagles on a beautiful day before more than 70,000 fans. Playing an arch rival that had just come off a Super Bowl year (they had lost to the Raiders) in their own stadium was a tall order for a Redskin team trying for its first win.

Neither team scored in the first quarter, but Philly scored a touchdown in the second period. Two Moseley field goals—one with a second to go—pulled us to within one, 7–6, at the half.

The Eagles scored a touchdown in the third period, but we matched that early in the fourth. Finally we were in a game for four quarters, trailing the previous year's league champion 14–13 with more than ten minutes to play. How I wish we had those ten minutes back. It was all Eagles from then on. A touchdown pass, a field goal, a safety, a field goal, and a fumble recovery in the end zone made it a 36–13 rout.

What can you say? What can you do? We had 23 first downs, 8 more than the Eagles. We had 337 net yards to their 221. Theismann had another good passing day. We even had possession more than five minutes longer. The problem was 22 fourth-period points by the Eagles. We were 0–4. To me it felt as if I personally was 0–4.

I had hardly ever faced a season where my team lost more than it won. It was a good thing I'd endured that disastrous 1978 season as offensive coordinator with

Tampa Bay, or I might not have had any idea how to handle this.

Everyone was frustrated. The media and the fans—many of them—decided that I was Jack Kent Cooke's folly. Their verdict was in: I should be out. I confess, every time I saw or heard from Mr. Cooke, my stomach tightened. He could have sent me packing, and he would have had every right.

The trouble was, I knew we had a good team. I had a feeling that if we could just break the barrier and get that first win under our belts, we would gain confidence and start showing what we could do. I have to hand it to Mr. Cooke. He stood behind me all the way. He even predicted we'd finish the season at least even. That looked like wishful thinking even to me at that point. I just wanted to win a game. I didn't want to be the first pro coach fired without winning at least one.

I gave it my best shot. If I was gone in a few weeks, at least I could say I reached the pinnacle of my profession. I may have failed, but it wouldn't have been for lack of trying. And I would have my yearbook to show that for one brief moment, not a very shining one, I had been an NFL coach.

At least our next game was at home. It did have to be against the San Francisco Forty-Niners, the eventual Super Bowl winners. They beat us up pretty good. Five of the first six scoring drives were theirs. They led 14–0 at the end of one, 17–0 early in the second, and 24–3 at the half. Going into the final period we trailed 30–3. Only a 58-yard punt return by Mike Nelms and a late 5-yard TD run by Joe Washington made the final score a bit more respectable at 30–17.

We'd had more first downs, more net yards, and even more time with the ball, but penalties, fumbles, and four interceptions killed us. Not to mention the Forty-Niners.

We were 0–5, and I was dying.

On the way home after that loss, the car was quiet. Pat was crushed, empathizing with me. J.D. was old enough to know that Dad wasn't in the mood for talk. Coy was fidgeting but quiet until we were about five miles down the road. I was staring straight ahead as I drove, scowling.

"Hey, Dad?"

"What?!"

"Where we gonna eat?"

Thank God for Coy! We may have been 0–5 and his dad may have been off to one of the worst starts in history, but, hey, we still had to eat!

It reminded me of a story I'd heard years ago about a coach who'd lost a game because of a missed extra point. He was in the pits, sitting on the couch, wallowing in misery. His wife came and sat beside him, gently took his hand, and reminded him how much he had to be thankful for. "You've still got me and the kids and we have this lovely home. I know it's awful to lose that way, but think of what you have."

And, just like a football coach, he was thinking, *Yeah, and I'd trade all of you for one extra point!*

When my secretary would tell me that Mr. Cooke was on the line, I'd jump two feet off the chair. But he was still encouraging. One day he came into the office with a couple of big notebooks under his arm. I had the feeling that when he got to me it would be time for the big meeting, the bad news. But all he told me, nodding at his notebooks, was that he was having trouble with "the tax people." He said he'd survive that and that the team would survive our disastrous start. Boy, I needed that. I don't know anyone who doesn't want to please his boss. My whole career I've wanted to more than please him, really. I want him to think I'm the best.

He said, "You wouldn't believe what people are calling me as they leave the stadium." But I would have. They were calling me worse.

When you lose one game, you see your weaknesses. When you lose two or three, you start to question your approach or your players. We're weak in this area; we're weak in that area. Five straight losses, and you believe you're dog meat. Yet here we were, 0–5, and I was still convinced we were a good football team. We had even made some good plays against San Francisco.

I kept trying to tell everybody how good we were. Most thought I was just trying to put things in a good light, but my coaches agreed with me. We had been able to tell what players were with us and who had already mentally bailed out. We didn't do a lot of shifting, but we did enough to know we had the right guys in the right positions. Something was going to click. We were going to start winning. We had to.

After five straight losses, winning becomes more than a goal. It becomes an obsession. It was then that I knew for sure that the horrible year in Tampa Bay had simply been part of my learning curve for being a head coach. I had discovered what it felt like and what it meant to lose and lose and lose, even when you were doing everything you knew to win. Had I become an NFL head coach in my thirties and without having had the Tampa experience, I can't say I wouldn't have panicked and done something stupid with an 0–5 start. I can't tell you how many times I thought about Tampa and realized that God had been preparing me for this. My goal now was to stand tight and strong and continue to make good decisions.

*We still believed we could
beat any NFL team,
but no one else
believed that.*

We still believed we could beat any NFL team, but no one else believed that. I also knew that the new staff had gotten to know each other in a way that success would not have made possible. We had seen each other at our worst, and like a first year of marriage when the honeymoon is over, we were discovering each other's true character.

Winning

We had a burning desire to beat the Bears in Chicago the next Sunday. In a way, being away from home took off a little pressure. No doubt the Bears and their fans looked forward to playing a team that hadn't won yet, but a team like that can often be dangerous, especially a good team. Their frustration can boil over into sloppiness or gutsy play. That day, finally, we put it all together.

Late in the first quarter the Bears stopped us deep in their territory and Moseley put us up 3–0 with a field goal. Twenty-four seconds later our middle linebacker, Neal Olkewicz, intercepted a pass at their ten and scored, and we went into the second period ahead 10–0.

Just before halftime we went up 17–0 on a John Riggins plunge. Our defense held until Riggins did it again late in the fourth period. It was too early to get overconfident, but we were hanging on at 24–0 with fewer than five minutes to play.

The Bears finally scored on a pass with a minute and a half left, but our four interceptions, Riggins's 126 yards rushing and our holding Walter Payton and Co. to 51 yards on the ground gave us a 24–7 win. We had done it!

We followed with a three-point loss to the Dolphins in Miami (they would finish the season atop their conference at 11–4–1). So, we were 1–6. If someone, anyone, had predicted that the Redskins would finish 1981 at 8–8 and win

35 of the 40 games after the Miami loss, he would have been put away forever. If there was one thing that propelled us into a record that few teams could ever match over the long haul, one thing that kept me from thinking that I or my system was good enough to take us to two straight Super Bowls, it was that 0–5 start.

That was a humbling, character-building motivator that had a dramatic effect on everyone in our organization. From the owner to the behind-the-scenes staff, we grew. We knew what we wanted and we had an idea how to do it. Sometimes negative motivation is the best. None of us wanted to endure a losing streak again, and we didn't lose more than two regular season games in a row again until November of 1988, my only losing season with the Skins (7–9).

We began our rise on October 25, 1981, when we took our 1–6 record into a home game against the Patriots. We won 24–22. The next week it was time for revenge against the Cardinals. We had another great day offensively and doubled them, 42–21. The following week we edged the Lions 33–31. We were now 4–6 and beginning to gain respect. The next week we paid back the Giants at their place, winning 30–27 in overtime. That was a crucial test. After four straight wins (three of them close) and five of our last six, we began to believe in ourselves. Best of all, we started to believe Mr. Cooke's prediction that we would finish the season at .500.

Two consecutive road losses, to the Cowboys and the Bills, almost killed our .500 chances. We would have to win the last three games of the season to finish 8–8. With a 15–13 edging of the Eagles and a 38–14 rout of the Colts, both at home, and a 30–7 win over the Rams in Los Angeles, we reached .500 on the last day of the season.

There would be no playoffs and little glory, but man, we had wanted that last win. We were playing for respect, for ourselves, and for our fans. We had gained more than 500 net yards to the Rams 165 and possessed the ball four full minutes longer. By now we knew we had a good team and that the 0–5 start was, if not a fluke, at least only a glitch in an otherwise winning organization.

> # There would be no playoffs
> ## and little glory, but man, we had wanted that last win.

What we had to prove to everyone else now was that we were the team that had finished the season 8–3, not the team that had begun it 0–5. I can't imagine a team ever looking forward to the next season with as much excitement as we did. No one could know then that it would be shortened by a player strike.

I knew by the end of that first roller coaster season that God had been preparing me for that all my adult life. The Tampa experience clearly had been necessary. Even my not getting a college head coaching job was important in His overall scheme. I had not been ready. I had not experienced enough. And when I *was* ready, I was ready for the NFL.

Of course, those first five weeks of the regular season had made it look like I was *not* ready for the pros. When I look back it sometimes still amazes me that Mr. Cooke stood by me as long as he did. But he's not just an owner; at least he's not a typical owner. He knows the game. He can see the nuances. He could see how hard we were working, that we had the right idea, that the team was coming together. We hadn't panicked. We had stuck to the fundamentals. Something told him that the 0–5 start was not the sole responsibility of the head coach. He predicted we'd finish at .500, and we did. He had no predictions for 1982. No one could have predicted what happened.

The pre-season didn't help the debate. We began with a 24–7 loss at Miami. Don Shula's Dolphins are always tough, especially at home, but we weren't happy with our sputtering offense. The press and our fans seemed to say that pre-season doesn't mean much anyway. We agreed, because we care more about assessing our talent and experimenting with our offensive and defensive alignments. Still, you like to win for the sake of momentum.

When we lost at Tampa Bay 28–13, we were still struggling on offense, and we had given up a lot of points. Pre-season still didn't mean much, everybody said, but we weren't supposed to lose to the Buccaneers, especially by two TDs.

The next week we played our only home pre-season game and lost 20–14 to the Buffalo Bills. I felt the coaches and players were keeping their heads about them, but being 0–3 in August made the previous year's regular season start all too fresh in people's memories.

When the Bengals put a 28–21 finishing touch on our pre-season in Cincinnati the following week, there was nowhere to hide. Fans and press noted that we had given up twenty or more points in each game. No one seemed to notice that our own point production had improved each week: 7, 13, 14, 21. All they knew was that we had a penchant for losing in streaks, and they didn't like it. Practice, exhibition, whatever. In the long run, they don't care if the games count or not. They want more wins than losses, and they're impatient with consecutive L's in the win-loss column.

I had a problem that would only be solved with time. I knew we had a good team, a very good team, maybe even better than that. Over the years you learn to notice things. We had the horses. And the players had the right attitudes. We coaches worked them hard, and they kept coming back for more. They believed in themselves. They weren't letting the pre-season numbers get them down. That 0–5 start the season before had shown us who had the heart and the guts to hang in and give peak performances regardless of our record or the circumstances. We wanted players who didn't care if we were favored or not, who didn't care about our record or the record of our opponent. If we had lost several games in a row and the team we were to play was the defending Super Bowl champ, our guys would not roll over and play dead.

I knew that, and I believed we could beat anybody in the league. I wasn't one for predictions or boasting, but secretly I believed not only that we *could* win a lot, but also that we were going to. Only the unfolding of the season would prove that, but strike rumors clouded everything.

Meanwhile, I was learning another lesson about investments. I thought I had known a lot about money, even though up until that time I hadn't had much of it. Whatever arrogance I had about my coaching ability had been taken care of by my new commitment to Christ and the Tampa Bay and 0–5 experiences. But I still thought I was a pretty shrewd businessman.

A friend of mine had been running short of money in an oil lottery deal, and he wanted me to get in it with him. He believed it would pay off some day, but he needed a partner. I liked him, but I thought the deal sounded too risky. I gave myself an out by saying that I had already talked Pat into a deal that failed and that I didn't want to bypass her counsel again. That was truly a brilliant thing to say, if I had meant it. There is safety, I know now, in having your spouse in full agreement. But back then I was saying that only because I didn't like the venture and didn't have the guts to say so. Oh, I wanted to take the risk, but I knew Pat would see it for what it was. I mean, an *oil* lottery? I thought, *Hey, there's no way in the world!*

Our friend got an expert to come and talk to us, and as

he was unfolding this grand scheme, I was snickering. I just knew that after our racquetball fiasco, Pat would want nothing to do with a pipe dream like this. He finishes and I'm trying to hide my amusement. Pat stands and says, "I think we ought to do it."

I was astounded. Just that quickly I went from skepticism to fascination. Maybe I was a sucker, but her optimism was all I needed. We sank a few thousand into the deal, and two months later we quintupled our money.

There was a very clear lesson in that. It was no formula, no guarantee, but I should have learned just one more time that my wife's counsel is valid, even in areas where she claims no expertise. Call it intuition, call it being attuned with God, call it wisdom. Whatever, the dynamic appears to be the agreement. I wanted to gamble on the oil lottery, but I didn't want to talk her into something again. It sounded like a long shot even to me, and it was. But I like to take those kinds of risks. I hid behind her to get out of it; she surprised me, and so did the payoff. Did I learn a lesson? 'Fraid not, as you'll see later.

One of the great rivalries in the National Football League is between the Philadelphia Eagles and the Washington Redskins in the NFC East. We have played them twice a season almost every year since the inception of the Redskins, more than a hundred regular season games. It has always been a home and away set before packed stadiums. Regardless what the respective teams had done before those games, it was all out the window at kickoff. For many fans and players, those were the games of the year.

We began the 1982 season September 12 at Philadelphia. They were a good team, the memory of their January, 1981, Super Bowl loss still fresh. After our pre-season, it was put up or shut up time for us. Their big guns were quarterback Ron Jaworski, halfback Wilbert Montgomery, wide receiver Harold Carmichael, and kicker Tony Franklin. We countered with Joe Theismann at quarterback,

John Riggins at fullback, Art Monk at wide receiver, and kicker Mark Moseley. Our defense was anchored by Dave Butz, Dexter Manley, and Neal Olkewicz.

This was an afternoon game in the sun, temperature in the low eighties, and it was a game to end all games. The Eagles took a 7–0 lead early on a short run by Montgomery. Late in the first period, Franklin made it 10–0 Eagles on a 44-yard field goal.

We took a 14–10 lead late in the second quarter on two short Theismann passes, one to Monk with two and a half minutes to play in the half (the eleventh play of an 87-yard drive), and the other to Charlie Brown. With one second on the clock in the second quarter, Franklin hit another 44-yard field goal to bring the Eagles to within one, 14–13.

The third period was all Eagles. All Montgomery, I should say. Four and a half minutes into the second half he capped an 8-play, 86-yard scoring drive with a 2-yard plunge. Four minutes later he caught a 42-yard TD pass from Jaworski. The Eagles led 27–14, and many wondered if we were going to be a first half team again, as we had been at the start of the season before.

We needed something dramatic, so we took a drastic gamble early in the fourth period. We took possession at our own 22-yard line and went for broke on first down. Theismann hit Brown with a 78-yard scoring strike, and though we still trailed 27–21, our fire had been lit. Our defense was inspired. Midway through the final quarter they gave us the ball at the Eagle 48, and five plays later Riggins ran the ball in and Moseley added the extra point to put us up 28–27. It was the second time we had led.

With less than three minutes to play, we threatened again, hoping to ice the game with a touchdown. With their fans screaming, the Eagles held us and made us kick a field goal. We now led 31–27, but we hadn't heard the last from Philadelphia.

Moseley, who had already scored seven points on three PATs and a field goal, booted the ensuing kickoff deep, and we tackled the ball carrier at the Eagle 10-yard line. We liked our chances. The Eagles needed more than a field goal to stay in the game, and they had ninety yards to go.

Eleven plays later, with 1:04 left on the clock, Carmichael caught a four-yard Jaworski pass in the end zone and Franklin added the extra point, his tenth point of the game. The Eagles led for the third time, 34–31, and now the onus was on us. Could we get close enough for a tying field goal?

With a brilliant hurry-up offense, led by Theismann, we moved 33 yards in seven plays and called time with one second left in the game. Moseley lined up for a 48-yarder that would give him ten points for the game. He made it. What a game!

In overtime, on our second possession, we moved 62 yards on eight plays, giving the ball to Mark again, this time for a 26-yard chip shot. Seeing that ball split the uprights was one of the thrills of my career. Man, we needed that game, and what a way to get it! The lead had changed hands six times, and we had beaten a great team in their own stadium. The pre-season was forgotten. The Skins were undefeated, leading the NFC East. Though we were only 1–0, we knew something important had happened. We had turned a corner and picked up momentum. How far it would carry us, we didn't know. But we were on our way to big things, we could sense that.

The game had been wonderful. We'd made 26 first downs to their 25. Both teams had over 400 net yards. The Eagles had made one more offensive play than we had, 71–70, though we held the ball seven minutes longer. Each team had four touchdowns, though we, of course had one more field goal. The kickers alone had accounted for 23 points. Our Riggins had rushed for 66 yards, their Montgomery for 63.

Theismann had completed 28 passes for 382 yards, while Jaworski had completed 27 for 371 yards. You could hardly ask for a more even game. Now it was on to Tampa Bay to try to avenge our pre-season loss to the Buccaneers. The question was whether we could get it in before the looming player strike.

Now it was on to Tampa Bay to try to avenge our pre-season loss to the Buccaneers. The question was whether we could get it in before the looming player strike.

On a Roll

Ball control was the name of the game in Tampa the next week, where we won 21–13. We had the ball nearly thirteen minutes longer than the Bucs, and Riggins ran for 136 yards. Theismann had a mediocre passing day, but so did Tampa's Doug Williams. In any other game I would have been proud to see my old friend Doug throw a 62-yard TD pass, but not against us.

By then we already had a 9–0 lead on a Theismann to Brown touchdown pass and a Moseley field goal. Both teams had missed their first extra points, and 9–6 was as close as Tampa came to us. Moseley had two more field goals, giving him seven in the first two games. Curtis Jordan recovered a fumble in the end zone for us in the fourth quarter. The Tampa fans had gotten excited early in that last period when their fullback, James Wilder, bulled in from the seven and the extra point brought them to within five at 18–13. But we held them the rest of the way and added a late field goal for the final score.

We were 2–0 and psyched up, but we wouldn't play another game for two months. Due to a strike by the NFL players' association, seven games were canceled. I tried to stay out of the controversy. I have always been pro-players, but they and I had to face the fact that I was management. All I asked was that they stay together as a team. We worked hard for that chemistry, and I just

141

wanted to be sure that nothing came between them. There was already a rift between them and league, of course. That couldn't be helped now. Our success as a team depended on how closely knit they could remain.

In the end the players' association achieved very few of its goals. Free agency was postponed for five years, and what they did gain benefited only about a third of the active players.

By the time the league reorganized itself for the rest of the year there was time for only seven more regular season games. We would play the Giants and the Cardinals twice each, the Eagles again, the Cowboys, and the Saints. Four of our games would be at home. We liked our chances. Though teams would take nine-game records into the post season, there would be AFC and NFC playoffs leading to the Super Bowl, as usual.

We jumped off to a 21–0 lead in a road game against the Giants, led 24–10 going into the final period, and won 24–17. Moseley had two more field goals and three extra points. Though net yardage was almost even between the two teams, the Giants had the ball nearly nine minutes longer.

The next week we had another close one against the Eagles, this time at home. We built a 10–0 lead, saw them come back to within one at 10–9 in the third period, but added a Moseley field goal near the end of that quarter. We hung on to win 13–9. The city was starting to catch the fever. The Redskins were 4–0, undefeated in a strike-shortened season.

When Dallas came to town December 5, 1982, we thought we were ready. We weren't. They held us scoreless for the first three quarters and went into the fourth period with a 17–0 lead. We battled back with a quick field goal and a Theismann to Brown TD pass to pull within one touchdown of them with almost ten minutes to play. But a 46-yard touchdown run by Ron Springs with less than a minute on the clock put the game out of reach. We lost, 24–10.

We made mistakes and we weren't happy with our performance, but I couldn't complain about desire and hustle. This had just been one of those times when a tough opponent comes in prepared and motivated and executes a beautiful game plan. The question now was how we would bounce back. I knew we weren't the kind of a team to go in the tank after a hard loss. Now we had to prove it. Would the Redskins start a multiple loss slide and fade from play-off contention? Or were we for real?

Our 12–7 win over the Cardinals in St. Louis the following Sunday was a testament to our kicking game and their defense. Their Ottis Anderson ran for more than a hundred yards against us, but they didn't score until late in the game after we had managed one field goal in each quarter. Moseley just kept motoring along, hitting four of four from 32, 30, 20, and 24 yards. That gave him eighteen straight field goals, two short of Garo Yepremian's record.

We had to rely on Mark again the next week when the Giants came to Washington, looking for revenge. It was a cold, blustery December 19 afternoon. Moseley scored our only points in the first half with a second period field goal, and we trailed 14–3 going into the locker room.

It snowed during the entire second half. In the third period Joe Washington ended a 10-play, 80-yard drive for us with a 22-yard touchdown run. Still we trailed by five, 14–9, going into the final period. Moseley kicked a 31-yard field goal with just over nine minutes left, and then we got him close enough to bang home the winner from 42 yards out with just four seconds to play. It was his record-breaking twenty-first straight, and we won, 15–14. If our dramatic opening victory over Philadelphia hadn't convinced people, this one sure did.

That game proved that some statistics can be misleading. We topped the Giants in first downs, 20–11, net yards 375–139, passing yards 252–128, and time of possession 38:19–21:41. Yet we won by one point on a last second field goal.

Also in that game, John Riggins carried 31 times for 87 yards and became only the fifth player in NFL history to carry the ball more than 2,000 times in a career. The other four were Walter Payton of the Bears, O.J. Simpson of the Bills, Jim Brown of the Browns, and Franco Harris of the Steelers.

Now we were 6–1 with two games to go, and we were smelling play-offs.

At the Louisiana Superdome in New Orleans, December 26, Moseley extended his streak with two more field goals (from 36 and 45 yards) as we beat the Saints 27–10. We dominated them 448–197 in total yards and 250–77 in yards passing.

We went into the last game of the season (at home against the Cardinals, Sunday, January 2, 1983) with a chance to win the home field advantage throughout the play-offs. We were proud of having allowed only 128 points in the previous eight games. A good defensive game would assure us the lowest points-against total in the NFL.

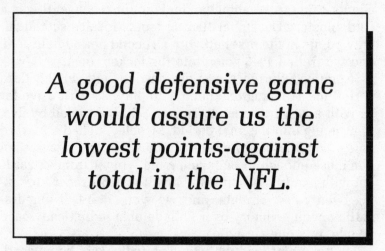

A good defensive game would assure us the lowest points-against total in the NFL.

Three weeks before, we had beaten the Cardinals by just five, and they wanted this one badly too. But the home field advantage was a tremendous motivator. We scored one touchdown and an extra point in each of the quarters on three passes from Theismann and one plunge. We held the Cards scoreless for a 28–0 win, the Skins first shutout victory since they had beat the same team 23–0 in

1980. We were in the play-offs for the first time since 1976, when Washington had lost 35–20 to Minnesota in the first round. Sadly, Mark Moseley had seen his field goal streak end, going wide to the right on a 40-yard attempt. It had been quite a ride for Mark, and we were all proud of him.

Because of the strike, there were no weeks off before or during the play-offs. And as long as we kept winning, we would be at home until the Super Bowl, which was set for the Rose Bowl in Pasadena, January 30. Three tough games stood in our way.

The first was Detroit on January 8 at RFK Stadium. We built a huge lead on them from the beginning. Jeris White, our corner back, intercepted a pass and ran it back 77 yards for our first touchdown, midway through the opening period. Moseley added a 26-yard field goal, also in the first. The next three scores were all ours and all similar. Theismann hit wide receiver Alvin Garrett on touchdown passes of 21, 21, and 27 yards, two in the second period and one in the third to put us up 31–0. Detroit finally scored on an Eric Hipple to David Hill pass late in the third quarter, but that was the end of the scoring. John Riggins rushed for 119 yards.

That game was another statistical surprise. The Lions had actually made more first downs than we did and were almost even with us on net yardage. But only one statistic counts at the end of the game, and we owned that one, 31–7.

In the other NFC first round games, Green Bay beat St. Louis 41–16, Dallas beat Tampa Bay 30–17, and Minnesota beat Atlanta 30–24. We would play Minnesota, and Dallas would play Green Bay.

In the first round in the AFC play-offs, Miami had beat New England 28–13, the Raiders beat Cleveland 27–10, the Jets beat Cincinnati 44–17, and San Diego beat Pittsburgh 31–28.

Minnesota was no easy opponent. They had a winning tradition, having appeared in four Super Bowls (losing all four) from 1970–77. On a cold and windy January 15, 1983, John Riggins nearly single-handedly won the game for us.

All the scoring was done in the first half, two-thirds of ours in the first period. We jumped ahead 14–0 on a 3-yard pass from Theismann to tight end Don Warren and a Riggins plunge. After the Vikings came back with a second quarter touchdown run by Ted Brown, Theismann hit Garrett with an 18-yard TD to give us a 21–7 lead that never changed. While Riggins had scored only the one touchdown, he had rushed 37 times for 185 yards and a play-off record, helping us hang onto the ball nearly ten minutes longer than the Vikings. When I finally took him out of the game, the crowd gave him a huge ovation. He deserved it. He had been a huge factor for us all year. As they rose, he stopped and bowed deeply in all four directions. It was just another example of John's impeccable timing. He always knew what to say and how to act before the public, and it endeared him to them.

Now we had the chance to play Dallas for the NFC championship. They had beaten Green Bay 37–26 and were the only team we had lost to all year. We could have worried about that, but our guys wanted revenge. We wanted the Super Bowl most, but it didn't bother us that it was the Cowboys who stood in the way. If we couldn't get past them, we didn't deserve the Super Bowl.

Meanwhile, in the AFC, the Jets beat the Raiders 17–14 and Miami beat San Diego 34–13. Those two winners would play for the AFC championship and the right to meet in the Super Bowl the winner of our game against Dallas.

On January 22, 1983, I experienced the loudest, most deafening crowd noise in my career. Our fans at RFK had a level of intensity I had never heard before. They shouted at the top of their lungs, "We want Dallas! We want Dallas!" It seemed they stayed on their feet screaming the entire game. From the day I had first arrived in Washington I had been told by self-proclaimed experts that the most important thing for my job security was to beat the Cowboys. Just the Cowboys. Up to now, my teams had not beat them in three tries. (Nowadays my teams also have to beat New York and Philadelphia!)

Dallas got on the board first on a Rafael Septien field goal midway through the first period. We answered with a touchdown pass from Theismann to Charlie Brown late in the quarter and added another late in the second period on a Riggins plunge. We felt good about going into the locker room with a 14–3 lead, but we knew it was far from over.

While their quarterbacks, Danny White and Gary Hogeboom, were combining for 23 passes and 275 yards, Riggins was doing his thing for us, running for two touchdowns and another 140 yards. We traded touchdowns with the Cowboys in the third period, and they added another to pull within four at 21–17 going into the fourth. It was still anybody's game, anybody's NFC championship, anybody's trip to Pasadena.

Halfway through the fourth period, Moseley hit a 29-yard field goal to give us a full seven-point lead. Now it was time for the defense to suck it up and keep the Cowboys from marching down the field on us. This was what we had been pointing to all year, having lost only once to this very team.

Two plays later, when our right tackle, Darryl Grant, intercepted a pass at the Cowboy ten and ran it in for an insurance touchdown, the crowd knew we had done it— we would be going to the Super Bowl for the second time in ten years. The game was scoreless in the fourth and the final was 31–17. Our fans went crazy.

Miami had shut out the Jets 14–0 in the AFC final, so we would meet the Dolphins in Pasadena on January 30, shooting for the first Redskin world's championship in 40 years. The night before the game we moved the players to a quiet hotel in Pasadena, away from fans and relatives and distractions. I talked briefly to the team before we all went to bed.

Early the next morning I sat out on the balcony, enjoying a pretty, slightly overcast sky. I was nervous. This was my first Super Bowl, and part of me wondered how we had ever gotten this far. I'm not in the habit of letting my Bible fall open to see what's on the page. Usually I try to have a plan and go systematically through some passage or theme. But that morning I just let it rest in my hand. It opened to the story of David and how he fought Goliath with the confidence and assurance that the Lord God almighty was on his side.

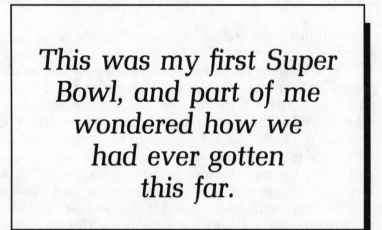

This was my first Super Bowl, and part of me wondered how we had ever gotten this far.

Well, I knew that God didn't take sides in football games, not even in Super Bowls. But I did take courage. *Why should I be afraid of a new experience? Why should I be afraid even of the mighty Miami Dolphins? If I belong to God, and David can kill Goliath, who knows? Maybe even the Redskins can beat the Dolphins.*

If someone would have told me that we would hold Miami to just 9 first downs while we racked up 24, that we would dominate them in net yards 400–176 and in offensive plays 78–40, that our average gain would be 5.1 yards to their 3.7, that John Riggins would run for another 166 yards, and that we would be ahead in time of possession 36:15–23:45, I would have predicted a huge blowout.

In fact, this was a frustrating, almost agonizing game we could very easily have lost.

Miami almost beat us on big plays alone, and if we hadn't held them scoreless in the second half, we would have been in real trouble. On the second play of a series near the midway point of the first quarter, David Woodley hit Jimmy Cefalo with a 76-yard pass that put them up 7–0. They held us scoreless for the first quarter, but just a few seconds into the second period, Moseley put us on the board with a 31-yard field goal. Uwe Von Schaman, their kicker, booted a 20-yarder of his own to make it 10–3, but then Theismann engineered an 11-play, 80-yard drive that ended with a 4-yard TD pass to Alvin Garrett. With less than two minutes to play in the first half, we had tied them at 10.

Fulton Walker returned the ensuing kickoff 98 yards and Miami took a 17–10 lead into halftime. Two freak—though admittedly perfectly executed—plays and a field goal made up the Dolphin scoring. We had ground out our one touchdown. My job at the half was to convince our guys that we were playing better football, that playing the way we were was the way to win big games. We couldn't blame anyone but ourselves and the talent of the Dolphins for the big plays that had us down, but if we stayed at the task and played good defense, we could wear them down and win.

I'm sure that wasn't news to the players, but I hoped they were pleased to know that I noticed. They'd been working too hard to be trailing 17–10. Now if they could gut it out for another half, things would turn for them.

With just under nine minutes to play in the third period, Moseley hit a 20-yarder that made it 17–13. Now we were within striking distance. We had to hold the Dolphins and keep moving on offense. Just before five minutes into the fourth period we had moved nine yards on three plays and faced a short fourth and one at the Dolphin 43. I had the best fullback in football in my backfield, and we were too far away for a field goal. A punt would have had to be perfect to not go into the end zone and see them set up at their own 20. We decided to go for it.

On fourth and one, Riggins powered all the way in to the end zone for a 43-yard touchdown. Replays of that tackle-breaking run have made it famous. Suddenly we had our first lead, 20–17. Late in the final period we drove 41 yards on 12 plays, the last of which was a 6-yard Theismann to Brown touchdown pass, that made the final score 27–17. The game was closer than the score looked and much closer than the stat sheet says it should have been.

But no matter which way you look at it, we were the Super Bowl winners, and we couldn't have been prouder or happier. What a journey it had been from 0–5 at the beginning of the previous season and 0–4 in the pre-season! Had it not been for those ordeals and the Tampa Bay experience just a few seasons before, I might have started thinking this NFL coaching wasn't such a mystery after all. I mean, you lose a few, then you get your system and your people in place and you start beating everybody. That's how it works, right? We can do it again next season, right?

I knew better. I knew that things change, breaks go both ways, injuries play no favorites. Lots of things can take you out of Super Bowl contention. Repeating was a long way from guaranteed.

I was amazed at the difference in how a coach is treated when he is losing compared to when he is winning. When I lost I was pitied, scorned, decried. When we put together a few winning streaks, and now that we had won it all, I was a genius. I was learning the easy way that the fans and the press can be fickle. At least I hadn't yet had to learn it the hard way.

I'd heard the fans scream at me to go for it on fourth-and-one. And I'd heard them raise the roof when I took the chance and succeeded. But I had also lost my head and gone for a fourth-and-one when it wasn't the right thing to do, and when it failed I heard them boo me for the very decision they had screamed for.

I realized that in life I'm always at fourth and one, and there are those who are urging me to go for it. Don't play it safe, don't play the percentages, don't do what your gut tells you is right. Do what we say, do what we want, take a chance. Go for it.

And you know what those voices were saying to me after that Super Bowl win? They were saying I was an okay guy. I was a pretty good football coach. I wasn't boastful or proud. I knew where I had come from, and I knew this would all be history the next time the Redskins came down to earth and started getting beat. But what about my security? I had a three-year deal. Sure, there was talk of extending it, but there are no guarantees in this life.

> *I realized that in life I'm always at fourth and one, and there are those who are urging me to go for it.*

Take the Super Bowl money and the increased salary, Joe. Do something with it. Make yourself secure. Invest. Be smart. Be wise. This may be all there is, the end of the rainbow. It's fourth and one and time to make your play.

I was humble about my coaching. I had a right to be. I believed I was made to be a coach, and I had seen my methods work. But I was realistic. In business? There I felt more confident even though I had *no* reason to. I had jumped into the racquetball deal against my wife's counsel and lost a lot of money. Then I would have avoided the oil lottery that eventually helped bail us out.

Now I had a chance to really do something for me and my family. My motive was pure. My intent was honorable. I was looking for a way to parlay this payday into something solid for my future, for the future of my loved ones. What could possibly be wrong with that?

Nothing. I was smart, shrewd. This could even be honoring to God. I would make the most of my resources.

Surely He could only honor that. The more I thought about it, the more I liked the idea. I wasn't sure what it was yet, but I would find a way to secure my future.

I basked in the adulation of Washington—as we all did —for as long as it lasted. There's nothing like being a winner and being known as a winner. Now it was time to excel in another field, the financial arena, one area that could really give our family security.

Capital
Offenses

It would be nice to have had so many Super Bowl appearances that you can't differentiate one from the other in your memory. But I'll never forget the first.

My mother and dad and my Aunt Louise were in the stands. Aunt Louise was so proud of me that her enthusiasm bubbled over, and within two minutes everyone around her knew why she was there and what her connection was to one of the head coaches. And if they found that hard to believe, she introduced them to my dad!

As the game progressed and the crowd got more and more boisterous, they tell me Dad was turning away autograph-seekers. But when we won, sure enough, he was standing there with a crowd around him, signing for everybody! Hearing about that was one of my biggest kicks from that whole experience.

Another of my sweet memories of that game was when I whirled around to find J.D. behind me as the final gun sounded. I bent and kissed him on the forehead, and someone caught that on film. It's one of my favorite pictures.

John Riggins won the Super Bowl MVP trophy and joked in the locker room, "Ron may be President, but for tonight, I'm king!" Boy, what a job he did for us with four straight one-hundred-yard plus games in the play-offs. He deserved every honor.

When we got back to Dulles Airport the next day, President and Mrs. Reagan were waiting for us, and that was just the beginning of the festivities. Half a million fans celebrated downtown in a heavy rain, February 2. When it was my turn to speak I held the trophy up and said, "This is for you!"

I was named Coach of the Year, which was a thrill. But I was just as happy for the players who were honored. Mark Moseley was named MVP of the NFL by the Associated Press, and five Redskins were named to the Pro Bowl: Charlie Brown, Moseley, Mike Nelms, Tony Peters, and Joe Theismann.

> *I was named Coach of the Year, which was a thrill. But I was just as happy for the players who were honored.*

A lot of people ask me about my memories of Joe Theismann. They assume I remember most the great days, the big passing games, the victories, the Super Bowls. Joe was a brash, driving, gutsy player who backed up everything he said. He has turned some people off, but you forgive a lot of that when a guy produces. And Joe was a producer, no question.

Fact is, my most vivid memory of Joe was not from one of the glamour games. It was that frozen, tough, hard day, December 19, when we played the Giants at home—the game in which Moseley broke the field goal record. It's a good thing he did or we would have lost. It was the day we beat the Giants on his last second kick, 15–14. It was fantastic, a powerful boot against the wind that put us in the play-offs.

Anybody who knows the game knows that it's the quarterback and the offense that gets you in position to kick those field goals. Moseley was a great kicker and deserves all the accolades he got, but that game was also the epitome of Theismann at his best, Joe doing it the only way he knew how.

He would throw four interceptions that day, three in the first half. He'd been hit hard several times and been rocked to that solid, icy turf. Late in the first half he got blind-sided by a linebacker and two of his front teeth were broken right in half. I stood on that sideline, looking at him kneeling there, spitting blood, and I was ready to give him a break.

The normal quarterback would have been looking for help. The average guy would have said, "That's enough for today. I've had it. Let somebody else take this. I'll come back and fight another day."

Not Joe. That guy came back in the second half, trailing 14–3, and led us down the field several times. Despite one more interception, he was 25 for 38 and 252 yards. That's what I remember most about Joe Theismann.

I know lots of people said he talked too much, but that was just Joe. Again, you can forgive a lot when a guy is willing to give his all.

Since his playing days, Joe, as a broadcaster, has predicted that I would soon leave coaching because I was burned out and had left my team void of player leadership. He has a right to say what he wants, but I have to say that hurt—both me and the players. I know, too, that I hurt Joe when he broke his leg a few years later. I called him several times, but I never made it to the hospital to see him. If I had it to do over, I'd have gotten there. I'd hate to think that's still coming between us. He was one of the greats, and he was sure the key to a lot of our winning seasons.

What I remember about Joe is similar to what coaches

remember about most players. It isn't always the Super Bowls. You don't remember only the great times and the great plays. You remember the tough times, when the guys stood against the odds and their hearts wouldn't let them back down.

Those are the same guys whose hearts won't let them believe it when their careers are over. I have to say, that is the other part about head coaching I knew nothing about until I got into it—telling a guy in his thirties that his career is over. The first part—feeling responsible for everyone on the staff and the team when things are going bad—I learned the hard way when we went 0–5. The second, being the guy who had to tell players when it was over, became an annual thing.

Boy, I hate that. I still have to do it, of course. I find myself talking to men I signed as boys. They were once young and virile and had no limitations. They were big and strong and fierce. The world was before them. They won a Super Bowl, maybe played in two. They were all pro. They made huge dollars. And now here they sit, old before their time, across from this guy they gave heart and soul for, and he's telling them it's over.

They don't believe it. They don't want to believe it. Their minds tell them they still have the quickness and the agility, that they're better than the rookies they see in the locker room and on the field. But their bodies deceive them, let them down.

Ironically, they are in magnificent shape for their ages and for what they have been through. They can still run and hit and block and tackle, and they would embarrass a neighborhood guy the same age. But being able to play at ninety percent of what you used to doesn't cut it in the NFL. The players are bigger and stronger and faster than they've ever been, and more eager and hungry-eyed lions flood into the system every year.

I won't delegate the job of telling him. I look him in the eye and I see that kid fresh out of college now imprisoned in an old man's body. He knows what's coming, but he hopes and prays against it. He might even argue. He might cry. Where else but in professional sports are men that young told that their careers are over? I hate it. I just hate it. Some of them never forgive me.

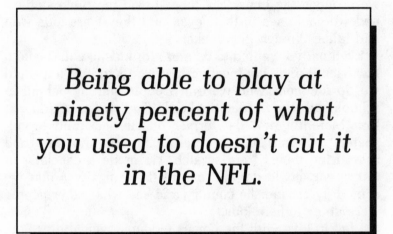

Being able to play at ninety percent of what you used to doesn't cut it in the NFL.

But it doesn't make sense for them to keep playing. They've already been to the mountaintop. Why come back and play as a second-stringer, a backup, for less money? Go out on top. But they look me in the face and say, "I can still play. I can still contribute." My job is to disagree. Some of them I thought I knew and trusted and considered friends have become my biggest critics. That just amazes me. I don't understand it.

I had been involved in ministering to troubled teenagers wherever I had been before, and I wanted to do something like that in Washington. I mentioned that desire in Sunday school a couple of years after I came to the Redskins. One of the men in the Sunday school class said he had two homes downtown where he took care of kids while they were being processed to go into the court system.

Several members of that class got involved in those homes for a couple of years. We had a Sunday morning Bible study. At first I took football films with me, because I couldn't imagine troubled kids sitting still for just preaching and teaching. But eventually I realized I was wrong. My practice had been to show the film and finish up with the Bible study, but after the first couple of weeks we dropped the films. The teens loved the Bible studies, and we could see in their eyes that they were kids who had fallen through the cracks.

Eventually I wanted to do more for kids like that, and a few friends and I got together to pray about it. What could we do for teens who were in trouble, getting behind in school, and who needed the Lord? That's where I first met Don Meredith (not the former quarterback and broadcaster), who had started several churches and was good at starting things from scratch. He made a checklist of things we should do, and one of the things was that we should fly around the country and see what other people were doing to help kids.

I fell in love with the homes Olympic weightlifter Paul Anderson had started in Dallas. Roger Staubach and Tom Landry were on the board, along with Dallas Mavericks' owner Don Carter and others. A man named Jerry Campbell was running the homes. Those men agreed to help and advise us if we started a similar home in Washington.

We started with a fundraising banquet, asking then Vice-President George Bush and Roger Staubach to speak. We booked one of the big hotels downtown that could seat 1,500 for dinner. About a month before the event I panicked, fearing we would have an embarrassingly small crowd. Many volunteers went to work, publicizing the dinner and inviting people, and on the big date every seat was filled. It was a fantastic night where we raised more than $150,000 for Youth For Tomorrow.

We found a 137-acre piece of property in the country, something I thought would be perfect for a youth home, but would otherwise never amount to much as an investment. We got it for $320,000, and today it's worth six or seven million.

After we made the down payment and showed the plans to a firm for the development of the ground, we were told that the dirt work alone would cost about $800,000.

But the heavy construction guys took it upon themselves and did all that work for nothing. With people chipping in services and money from all over, we built about a $1.5 million facility without debt.

We then started bringing in kids, and we've had about 125 go through the program. They go to the on-campus school year around to catch up on their studies. We have full-time live-in parents in each of three wings, which house eight or nine kids per wing. We have taken no government funds, so we are free to start the day with prayer and Bible study and teach godly principles. It's nondenominational, and our desire is that every kid that comes in there leaves with a personal relationship with Jesus Christ.

Another goal is to get them through high school and either back home, into the service, into college, or into the work force. We try to keep up with them after they've left. It's been a tremendously rewarding part of our lives. I'm on the board, Pat works with the women who do a lot of fundraising (we have to raise about $800,000 a year), and I try to get to the home to be with the boys as much as I can. The home still has no debt, and the Lord has provided just enough for us to keep going, which is fantastic. But our dream is to have a couple more homes and an educational and athletic campus.

Our own boys were getting older, J.D. getting into high school sports and Coy a few years behind him. Now I could really enjoy life. Watching my kids play Little League and all the other sports was even more thrilling to me than winning the Super Bowl. I know that sounds crazy, but most dads will know what I'm talking about. Seeing your own son smack one over the fence or make a game-saving tackle or run a touchdown is one of the great thrills of life. I remember those details more than I can remember the big plays in more than ten years of NFL coaching, including the Super Bowls.

How can I forget Coy being so excited and so determined to please his coach that he would get sick before a game, then wear himself out running the plays in from the coach to the quarterback the whole game? He would be absolutely exhausted, drained at the ends of those games!

> *Watching my kids play Little League and all the other sports was even more thrilling to me than winning the Super Bowl.*

J.D. had wanted badly to be an impact player, a quarterback or running back. He begged me to let him go out for football at an age when I'd rather have had him wait. I let him and then discovered that he had been put at center. He wasn't going to complain after talking me into letting him play. He gave it all he had.

When he was a freshman in high school he went to an all-star game and played quarterback for the first time in his life. The starter had been hurt and the coach told me later he had made the difficult decision of going with J.D., a kid with no experience at the position. J.D. did the best he could, which wasn't bad for a freshman, but he took some good lickings. It was then that I realized there was a price to pay being the son of a pro coach. It wasn't all roses.

He would be sacked and in pain, and the defenders would say, "Take that back to your dad, Gibbs!"

By the end of the game J.D. was in tears, but he never quit. It broke my heart to hear about that. The coach apologized to me for having to use him like that, "But you know," he said, "he's going to be a good quarterback some day. He's got what it takes."

He was right. J.D. went on to have a good high school career as a quarterback and get a scholarship to William and Mary. There he realized that he wouldn't play much until he was a junior or a senior if he waited in line at quarterback. So he volunteered to be a defensive back and played backup for a year and started for two.

Coy was a sensitive kid who thrived on encouragement. Football meant everything to him. I did what I could to see that he was put into an athletic program where he would get just that. I didn't want to be the typical know-it-all who intimidates his kids' coaches. I tried to stay out of things. But when I saw that he was unappreciated or misunderstood, I took his side. Eventually I would get him into a high school where he could shine, and he would go on to win a scholarship to Stanford as a linebacker.

One thing I was very aware of after the Super Bowl was that the next year could be a disaster. I was simply being realistic. Basically I'm an optimist. I would be shooting for another Super Bowl, of course, but no one could predict injuries or bad breaks. I was in the third year of a three-year contract, and if we had a bad season, who knew whether I'd be back? Who knew whether I'd be anywhere? You'd think a coach who took a team to the Super Bowl would be able to get work somewhere, but at what salary?

The Super Bowl bonus money was the key to security. I was going to be smart. If things worked the way I hoped they would, I would be able to live without coaching if I had to. I didn't want to, but wouldn't it be nice if coaching could be a pleasant option in my life without being my main source of income?

My big break came when an old acquaintance from college days let me in on a wonderful opportunity. He was a builder operating in an area of the country where the economy was booming, people were moving in, and builders were making money. His plan was simple and lucrative. He would procure land and build homes, apartment complexes, and duplexes. He could borrow up to eighty percent of the value of these properties, but of course it cost him much less than that to build them.

For instance, if he built a place for sixty thousand dollars, it might be worth eighty thousand on the market. He could borrow eighty percent of that market value, or sixty-four thousand, see a little immediate profit, and rent out the place for cash flow that would more than pay the monthly mortgage installments. My part would be to put up as much capital as I could handle.

That was easy. A few thousand dollars in closing costs was the extent of my outlay, and then the rents would pay the monthly loan charges plus maintenance. It was too good to be true. I jumped in with both feet, visions of wealth in my head.

Let me be clear. My motive was not all bad. I was thinking of my family and our future. I talked for hours with my friend, getting all my questions answered and seeing the developments. The question wasn't whether I was interested; the question was how much liquid I could find to sink into this deal. I didn't need much. Super Bowl cash got us started and my financial statements made me a good candidate for mortgages—lots of them.

Pat was against the idea from the beginning, but this time she just had to be wrong. Where else could I get into so much real estate with so few dollars? Each property immediately began paying for itself. It was a cinch. I went into partnership with my old friend, he built, I signed, I paid, and the money began to roll in. Sure, I was heavily leveraged, but that was the kind of leverage I liked. I owned hundreds of thousands of dollars worth of property after having put up just three or four thousand in closing costs on each. All I had to do was make the payments, and the rent money would more than cover that.

I tried to be humble about it. I really did. I told hardly anyone. But what a businessman I had become almost overnight! I mean, sure, I'd made a few bad investments in the past. I'd lost money in the racquetball venture. I'd even lost on a nursing home deal. But this! This was big time.

With buildings going up, renters moving in, checks filling the accounts so mortgages could be paid, I could see that my only limit was time. How fast could my friend build? Sign me up for more. I wanted more.

Football coaching was fun, you know, and I was pretty good at it. But short-term contracts and your future rising on turns of fortune, that's no way to live. I couldn't imagine not coaching, but I wanted to get to the place where I didn't have to. When these rental places had been going for a while, our plan was to sell them. Investors would love the idea of income-producing properties, and we could sell them for much more than the original market value. Then my friend and I would split the take. First we had to build a huge base of properties. In a few years we would have a lot of properties to turn into big profits.

I knew what I was going to do with my take. I was going to buy more. Why hadn't I seen this before? It would have been worth borrowing to get into! I was a football coach and a real estate developer, if the truth was known. The more I accumulated, the better the thing looked. More and more rent money came in, and the mortgage and upkeep payments were easily covered.

Best of all, back then there were tremendous tax benefits from a deal like that. Almost every dollar I put in was tax-free or tax-deferred. One day I checked my resources and liked what I saw. I visited the development with my friend, made a quick tour, and invested in fourteen homes in one day.

I can't tell you how heady that was and how secure I felt. I didn't see it as arrogance. It was more glee, self-satisfaction. I had found the goose that lays the golden eggs. On my way back home I stopped in Fayetteville to see George Tharel and to let him share my good fortune. I shook my head and laughed. "I can't believe I bought fourteen homes today." Football was fun, but this was easy.

Pat was still wary. More than wary, she was against it.

She didn't share my excitement. She saw trouble on the horizon. During those few times when I allowed myself to think the unthinkable, that the bottom would fall out and I'd lose my money, I was still content. I believed I was the one person among the partners who could afford to lose his investment.

Of course that's the wrong way to look at an investment, because it's backward. The one who can afford to lose is the one who will lose, because if it goes sour, everyone else is broke and out of work. Their pockets aren't deep, and so who do the creditors go after? The one who thought he could afford to lose. The recognizable person. The visible one with a good job and steady income.

The more concerned Pat was and the closer it got to the next football season, the less I wanted to do with the business. I was still sold on it, but I knew I had to concentrate on football. I trusted my partner, things were going well, and I needed to get on with the Redskins. There was this matter of a Super Bowl championship to defend.

Not all of my investments were selfish. I had begun to fulfill my dream of a boys' home in the Washington area. And in the process of realizing that dream, I met Don Meredith. Don immediately impressed me as a soft-spoken and softhearted brother with a cool head and an articulate way of sharing ideas and truth. The more he worked with us, the more I liked him, and we struck up a friendship.

Don is a behind-the-scenes kind of a guy, not maneuvering for the limelight. He had good ideas, knew how to study something and make an educated proposal, and was generally the kind of a guy you like to have around when you're trying to get something done. I didn't know how good a friend he was until I put him to the test, but even before that I knew he was a special man and a godly man. (You can send me the check any time now, Don.) He and his wife Sally have become good friends of ours.

It was a good thing I knew Don and that he was the kind of man he was. Someday I would need him as I had never needed a friend before.

Going for Broke

Pretending to be an expert in business didn't last long. Now I wanted to be a passive investor. I let the partnership run things, and I merely provided capital and watched it grow. Outwardly I was the successful coach of the champion Redskins. Privately I was stockpiling wealth in a financial empire that required hardly any of my time. What a shrewd guy I was!

We finally figured out how to handle a pre-season schedule. If you win them all, you're expected to go undefeated for the season too. If you lose them all, your job is in jeopardy before the season even starts. We didn't do it on purpose, but in the 1983 pre-season, we won two and lost two. That gave plenty of ammunition to people who said the pre-season meant nothing and to those who said it meant everything. The fact was, despite a big loss to Miami at home, I liked what I saw. Privately, I believed we would be every bit as strong as we had been the year before.

The press made a big deal of our 12–1 overall record for 1982. It was our best record ever and the fifth best in NFL history. That was great. But if there's ever been a living example of what-have-you-done-for-me-lately?, it's the NFL. You're only as good as your last game and your present standing. It's a lot easier and even more fun to be a surprising upstart than a defending champion with no alibis. We still had Theismann and Riggins. We still had Moseley. We still had our receivers and our linemen and our running backs. There was no more time to relax and enjoy the praise. We had to do it again.

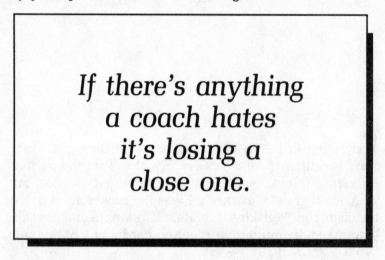

If there's anything a coach hates it's losing a close one.

If there's anything a coach hates it's losing a close one. You like to build up an early lead that changes the other coach's game plan, then put your defense to the test and hold on for the win. That game plan almost worked for our 1983 opener, a Monday night TV game at RFK against the Cowboys. Our rivalry was in full bloom now, and my good friend and fellow believer, Tom Landry, was roaming the other sideline. I respect that guy, and I loved to beat him, which I had done just once in four games.

We couldn't have started better if we'd scripted it ourselves. Of course we like to think we did, with our hours of game planning. A Moseley field goal and a Riggins TD gave us a 10–0 lead in the first period. Dallas came back with a field goal in the second quarter, but we added two Moseley field goals and a 41-yard pass from Theismann to Charlie Brown with half a minute to play in the first half. We led 23–3 and went into the locker room like champs. There were two quarters to go, but it had been eight regular season and play-off games since anyone had scored more than two touchdowns on us.

Until that night. The Cowboys came back out ready to work. While we sputtered, unable to put anything together until the final minute of the game, they racked up four straight touchdowns, two in the third period and two in the fourth. In the third, six minutes apart, Danny White hit Tony Hill with TD passes of 75 and 51 yards. We were still up by six at 23–17 until late in the fourth period when Danny White scored on a quarterback keep and less than a minute later we turned the ball over and they scored again to go ahead 31–23. Only a late touchdown pass brought us to within one, and we lost a heartbreaker we should have won, 31–30.

It didn't make any difference that we had had a stellar first half. It meant nothing that we had 91 more net yards and more than a hundred more passing yards. Theismann had gone 28 for 38 and 328 yards. We even had possession of the ball *fifteen minutes* longer than the Cowboys. But they won.

The point is to win, not to dominate the stat sheet.

The next Sunday at Philadelphia it was sunny and hot, 92 degrees at kickoff. We scored the first touchdown and the only one in the first half, but going into the fourth period we were tied at 10. With two field goals and a touchdown to their one field goal, we outscored them 13–3 in the fourth and won 23–13.

The following week we played the Chiefs at RFK, the first time Washington had faced them since a three-point loss in 1976. We stunk it up in the first half. Nothing was working, and the Chiefs' kicker, Nick Lowery, kept getting close enough for field goals. He made one of 58 yards (you read it right), then missed one from 47. In the second period alone he kicked field goals of 21, 32, and 22 yards. We were down 12–0 at the half and in danger of starting the season at 1–2. That was no way to follow up a Super Bowl. We were booed all the way to the locker room.

By the beginning of the third quarter the sun was blistering. It was humid and everyone was drenched. The

Chiefs' offense went into hiding and things started to gel for us. Moseley got us on the board with a 35-yarder, and a couple of minutes later Riggins rumbled in from the 2-yard line to give us the lead. A couple of touchdown passes and another field goal iced it for us. We had been outscored 12–0 in the first half, then turned around and outscored them 27–0 in the second half.

That kind of a turnaround helps you remember a game, but something else happened that afternoon that I'll never forget. It came in the third quarter when we were racking up two touchdowns and a field goal. The place was rocking and the fans were going crazy. I was thirsty, so while the players celebrated one of the scores, I worked my way back to the table where ten-year-old Coy was keeping track of the water and the Gatorade.

His job was to fill the cups and line them up so players and coaches could just reach for one whenever they needed it. Picture almost 53,000 people screaming, players high-fiving each other, me sweating and grinning and eager to get a drink. It was pandemonium. I felt like I had been on that field with my players, fighting my guts out.

I reached down for a cup and there was Coy at the back of the table, pretending two empty film canisters were cars. He was playing cars, oblivious to the sweat and the blood and the cheers and the uproar. It was almost as if a magnet made me stand there a second longer. I could hardly turn away.

Here I was in the middle of a big game, one that had just turned our way. It was the most important thing in my life. Yet here was truly my life, this little kid who couldn't have cared less whether I won or lost. I was stunned. His priorities had not been screwed up. He was having fun in his own little world. It hit me that there were millions of people all over the world who didn't know or care that the Redskins were playing the Chiefs. *Really*, I wondered, *where is the true perspective?*

The world says that right then nothing is as important as winning that game. To my son it meant little. And to me, what will mean anything twenty years from now? I may still remember that we won that game, but I may not. I know I'll remember Coy playing cars and showing me what was important.

> *It hit me that there were millions of people all over the world who didn't know or care that the Redskins were playing the Chiefs.*

We get all caught up in the externals of life, whether it's tennis or golf or business deals, and we run the risk of losing the things most important to us: our own kids.

That game against Kansas City had been one of those where we matched on first downs and total yards, but it was our ability to keep control of the ball for eight more minutes that gave us the win. Something that had already begun to impress me about our offense was that we were racking up points. In our last nine games, including two regular season games in 1982, three play-off games, the Super Bowl, and our first three in 1983, we had never scored fewer than 21 points and were averaging 27. Had I known what would happen the rest of the way, I would have been even happier. We scored 27 (20 in the first half) the following week against the Seahawks in Seattle, leading the whole way and winning by 10. We would not score fewer points than that in a game for the rest of the regular season.

The more we won—we were now 3–1—the worse was

the taste of that opening one-point loss to the Cowboys. They beat us. They deserved it. But when you've lost by one you can look at a dozen key plays that might have made a difference. I'm a big one for putting losses behind you and getting on with it, but it's not always easy. Our next game would be against the rugged L.A. Raiders at RFK on Sunday, October 2, 1983. We'd rather have gone in against them undefeated, but we still liked our prospects.

This was one of those games that makes a coach old before his time. We jumped off to a 10–0 lead by early in the second period, then we traded touchdowns to keep the ten-point edge, 17–7 at the half. What hurt us was a 99-yard touchdown pass from Jim Plunkett to Cliff Branch. You always hate to see that. It's like giving them seven points. Our defense doesn't break down on a big play like that and maybe we're still shutting them out at the half.

Mark Moseley extended the lead to 20–7 with a 29-yard field goal early in the third quarter, but just as Dallas had done in the opener, the Raiders awoke. With two touchdowns in each of the last two quarters, they stormed past us to take a 35–20 lead. With half a quarter to play, we were in deep trouble, needing two touchdowns and a field goal.

Plunkett had hit Calvin Muhammad with TD passes of 35 and 22 yards in the third quarter. And in the fourth he had found Todd Christensen in the end zone for a 2-yarder. What nearly nailed our coffin shut was Greg Pruitt's 97-yard punt return for a TD midway through the last period.

But the Skins were not to be denied that day. Theismann ended a four-play, 88-yard drive with an 11-yard pass to Charlie Brown in the end zone. With about five minutes to play, Moseley kicked a 34-yarder to make it 35–30. The defense rose to the occasion and got us the ball back late, and Theismann marched us 69 yards on five plays, the last a 6-yard scoring strike to Anthony Washington with about half a minute to play. We won, 37–35.

That's an exciting way to win a game, but you don't want to have games like that every week. Plunkett and

Theismann had really put on a show, throwing for 372 and 417 yards. But Joe threw no interceptions to Plunkett's four, and that made the difference.

We were 4–1 when we headed for St. Louis, where we finally got the breather we were looking for. It was not as easy as the score looks—it never is—but early in the second quarter we broke a 7–7 tie and scored 31 points by the end of the third period. We won 38–14 despite netting almost the same number of yards as the Cards and possessing the ball the same amount of time. There's no figuring this game.

We looked forward to the next Monday night when we would get a chance to show our stuff to a national TV audience at Green Bay. It would be one of the most entertaining Monday night games in history and by far the highest scoring. The lead would change hands six times, and we would control the ball more than a quarter longer than the Pack. Theismann would throw for nearly 400 yards and we would rack up ten more first downs. We would net 552 yards to their 473 and dominate in third-down efficiency.

But you already know better than to try to pick a winner from the stat sheet. This was one of those games we would think back on for years. Everybody who was in it, everybody who saw it, and even a lot of people who only say they were there, remember it as one of those games, the kind you tell your grandkids about. It was rock 'em, sock 'em, no holds barred, see-who's-still-standing-at-the-end football. It was what the game was designed for, and I wouldn't have wanted to be anywhere else.

Coach Gibbs discusses a play with running-back coach
Don Breaux. *(Scott Cunningham/NFL Photos)*

Gibbs gives last-minute instructions to Joe Theismann.
(Nate Fine/NFL Photos)

(Courtesy of Leader Enterprises)

Joe during a time-out with Don Breaux, offensive line coach
Jim Hanifan, and Charley Taylor.

(Richard Gentile/NFL Photos)

From left are defensive line coach Torgy Torgeson (with the Redskins
since 1971), Coach Gibbs, linebacker Greg Manusky, and center
Jeff Bostic, watching a play from the sidelines.

Number 17 Doug Williams (the first black quarterback in a Super Bowl game) and Charley Taylor (coach of the wide receivers) take quick orders from Coach Gibbs. With over 110 wins under his belt, they have reason to listen to Gibbs.

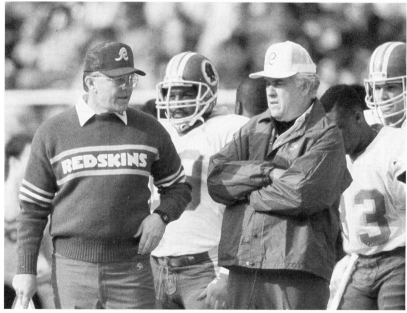

Running back Reggie Branch, Don Breaux, and wide receiver Ricky Sanders on the sidelines, waiting for a chance to show what the Skins can do. Their play-off record under Gibbs is one of the best in the league.

Legendary quarterback Joe Theismann (left) with Gibbs during
Super Bowl XXII in Pasadena.
(Courtesy of Leader Enterprises)

Jack Kent Cooke has given Gibbs free reign to take the Redskins all the way to the top. Gibbs has used his freedom to the team's advantage.
(Courtesy of the Washington Redskins)

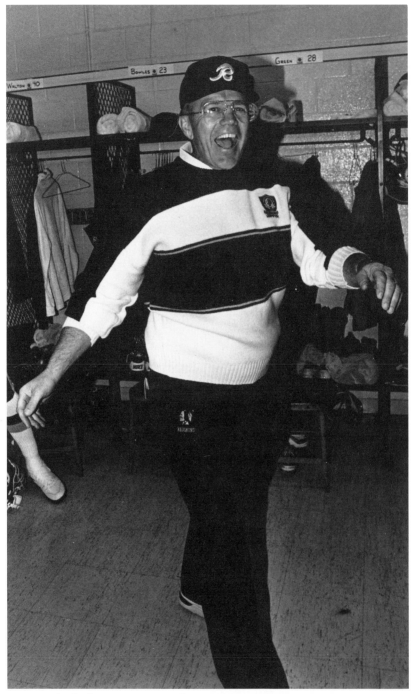

Everybody loves to win, and Joe is no exception. By 1990, Joe was
the fourth winningest coach among active NFL coaches.
(Courtesy of Leader Enterprises)

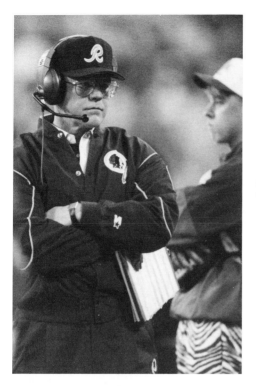

*Deep concentration and hard
work won Super Bowl XXVI.*

*Coach Gibbs paces the sidelines
during Super Bowl XXVI.*

Coach Gibbs salutes the players and fans
after defeating the Buffalo Bills, 37–24.

Coach Gibbs celebrates his victory,
coming home from his third Super Bowl win.

Onward

Any player or coach who tells you he is not aware of the difference between a nationally televised game and a locally televised one is kidding. We all try to tell ourselves that we play each game the same, that they all count equally, and that we give our all every minute, regardless. But no one in the NFL can tell me that he isn't aware when tens of millions more fans than usual are watching his every move. Maybe it's subconscious, but somehow players on both sides of the ball seem to be able to turn it up a notch for a game the whole country will see.

It was clear and chilly at Lambeau Field in Green Bay, Wisconsin, October 17, 1983, when we put our 5–1 record on the line against the Packers and before a nationwide "Monday Night Football" TV audience. A minute into the game their right outside linebacker Mike Douglass recovered a fumble and took it 22 yards into the end zone. A few minutes later our Clint Didier recovered a fumble in the end zone to tie the game.

Green Bay kicker Jan Stenerud and Mark Moseley traded field goals and we were tied at ten at the end of the first period. The night had just begun.

In the second period Packer quarterback Lynn Dickey hit Paul Coffman with a 36-yard touchdown pass, Riggins tied the game for us with a plunge from the one, and Dickey hit Coffman again from the nine to put them up

179

24–17. A Moseley field goal with two seconds left in the half brought us to within four at 24–20. The night was still young.

Fullback Gerry Ellis scored from 24 yards early in the third period to give the Packers a 31–20 lead. Every other score had been ours since the beginning of the game, but because three of ours had been field goals compared to only one of theirs, they held the 11-point lead.

Finally things started to go our way. With three consecutive scoring drives to close out the third period (two field goals and a Theismann to Joe Washington TD pass), we led for the first time, 33–31, with a quarter to go.

Early in the fourth, Green Bay took the lead again (38–33) on a 2-yard reverse by Gary Lewis. Four minutes later John Riggins punched the ball in from a yard out to put us up 40–38. No one had left the stadium. Two minutes later, Dickey hit Mike Meade from our 31-yard line, and the lead had changed hands again—Packers 45, Redskins 40.

We weren't finished. Theismann hit Joe Washington with a 3-yard pass in the end zone with less than two minutes to play, and we led 47–45. I have to hand it to the Packers; they never gave up either. They marched down the field and got close enough for Stenerud to put them up 48–47, with a 20-yard kick. Believe it or not, there was still enough time left for us to get the ball back and take it all the way down the field and try our own last second field goal. I believe it was the only kick Mark Moseley missed for a team I coached when the game was on the line. It was the highest scoring game in the history of Monday Night Football.

The game was a fan's and a statistician's delight. We and Green Bay had combined for 138 offensive plays for more than a thousand net yards and 56 first downs. There were 820 yards passing alone. It was the kind of a game you love to play and hate to lose.

The toughest part about that loss was that it was our second by one point. Again, something different happening in any one of a dozen plays might have made the difference; we had a 5–2 record that could have easily been 7–0. There was something about that game that was as motivating as our 0–5 start had been two years before. You kick yourself all week over the little things that might have changed the outcome, and you get tired of it. That's no way to live, and the only way to avoid it in the future is to be obsessive about the little things. It's one thing to get beat by a better or more prepared team; it's quite another to beat yourself or to lose by a point. From that time on, we were on a rampage.

The next Sunday we hosted the Lions and virtually beat them in the first half. Before a small crowd due to heavy rains, we scored four touchdowns in the first half to take a 28–3 lead, going on to win 38–17. With Riggins out with an injury, Reggie Evans came on to score three touchdowns for us. We were 6–2, and our offense was rolling.

The next Monday at Jack Murphy Stadium in San Diego, we had a real scare. After leading 10–7 at the half, we held the Chargers scoreless until midway through the fourth period while we added a couple of Riggins touchdowns. We felt pretty good about leading 24–7 with just over eight minutes to play. The next thing we knew we were down to two minutes and the Chargers' quarterback Ed Luther had thrown touchdown passes of 23 and 27 yards and Rolf Benirschke had booted a 43-yard field goal. After having dominated the game, we were now tied at 24. Mark Moseley, who had missed four field goals that day from between 39 and 52 yards, made one from 37 with nine seconds to play, and we salvaged the win, 27–24.

We were 7–2 and overdue for a big game. It came against the Cardinals in Washington on Sunday, November 6, 1983. We scored on a fumble recovery in the end zone late in the first period and never looked back. We led 17–0 at the half and 24–0 before the Cards scored their only touchdown, in the third quarter. We scored 21 in the third and 17 in the fourth to win 45–7 and run our record to 8–2. By now, everyone was taking notice. Our record and our play looked like a Super Bowl defending champion's. We were the team to beat and our sights were set on

Tampa Stadium for January 22. But there were a lot of games to be played before that. No one was going to hand us a trip to the Super Bowl.

We continued to roll with a 33–17 win over the Giants in New York the next week. John Riggins ran for 122 yards. We had led 16–3 at the half and 33–3 before the Giants scored a couple of late TDs. Pretty much the same thing happened the next week in Los Angeles against the Rams. We led 29–6 at the half and 42–6 in the fourth period before the Rams scored two touchdowns to make the final 42–20. Our defense had held Eric Dickerson to 37 yards rushing and Vince Ferragamo to 100 yards passing. We were 10–2.

Riggins had scored three touchdowns in that game, on his way to a record 24 for the regular season. It was his twelfth straight game with a rushing touchdown, another record. He extended the streak with two more the next week when our eleventh win came at home 28–24 over the Eagles. It was a game where we never trailed but where we led by as much as 28–14 at one point. Almost all the scoring came in the second quarter. We led 7–0 after the first period, then both teams scored three touchdowns in the second. You had to feel bad for their quarterback, Ron Jaworski, who threw for 333 yards in a losing cause.

The next week at home we ran our record to 12–2 by scoring the first 34 points against the Atlanta Falcons and winning 37–21. Despite 87 yards rushing for Riggins, he did not score and his streak ended at thirteen games in which he had scored at least one touchdown. Even without his personally pushing the ball across the line, our offense was on fire. We were also able to start resting people late in the game, crucial for post-season success.

I could have easily had an identity crisis by now. If I hadn't been through some rough times, I might have agreed with what the press was saying about me. We could easily have been 14–0, following a Super Bowl victory year. We would play the Cowboys in Dallas the next Sunday in a game that would determine the conference championship and home field advantage in the play-offs.

After the win over the Falcons I spent my one night of the week at home in my own bed, and to be honest, I was a little pumped on myself. I mean, I hadn't been in the NFL that long, and since that disastrous 0–5 start in 1981, my teams were 32–6. Maybe winning in the NFL wasn't all that big a deal after all—at least for a coach like me. Humble, wasn't I?

> *I could have easily had an identity crisis by now. If I hadn't been through some rough times, I might have agreed with what the press was saying about me.*

The next morning I got up to go to work and started thinking about the big game in Dallas the following Sunday. *Yeah, another day at the office with the brain trust, mapping out strategy for the battle.* Pat said, "Hey, pick up your socks and that bathrobe."

I thought, *The nerve of her! Does she realize who she's talking to?*

Then she tried to talk to me about what I considered a pretty mundane problem with one of the kids. *What is she doing? I've got all this important stuff on my mind and she's bothering me with that?*

I let her know somehow that I didn't have time to worry about anything just then and huffed out to the car. I had made a habit of praying on my drive to the office, but after that performance I didn't feel much like it. I forced myself, but that day the communication was coming from God rather than going to Him. In His own way, deep in my spirit, He was showing me who I was and who I wasn't.

By the time I got to the office I knew what I had to do. I called home. "Pat," I said, "I want to tell you something. What you're doing with the boys and what you're taking care of at home is more important than what I'm doing here at work. I just want you to know that I know that."

She's a good woman. She forgave me for being such a boor. It wasn't the last time she would have to do that.

When I got on the bus at Redskin park to head for the airport with the team, I was shocked to find our guys all dressed in battle fatigues for the trip to Dallas. If it was going to be a war, they wanted to be ready. I was worried about the impact it would have on the Cowboys, the press, and the fans. I would not have encouraged it, but it turned out to be a gutsy, motivating thing to do.

Two quick touchdowns in the first quarter set the tone, and we led 14–10 at the half. We kept in mind that we had led 23–3 at the half in the season opener at home against this same team and had lost 31–30. This time our offense kept connecting and our defense held in the second half. Tony Dorsett was held to just 34 yards for the game, one yard on five carries for the second half. We won 31–10 and took over sole possession of first place in our division. We were 13–2 with only the Giants remaining in the regular season.

They were tough. The next week four of the five scoring drives in the first half belonged to New York, all of those ending with field goals by their Ali Haji-Sheikh. We managed a lone touchdown in the second quarter and trailed 12–7 at the half. We traded touchdowns in the third and went into the final period down 19–14.

I didn't have to fire up my guys. Having lost just two games all season (by one point each), they didn't want to lose the last one whether it meant anything in the standings or not. We wanted momentum going into the play-offs. We outscored New York 17–3 in the final period to win 31–22 and took a 14–2 record into the post-season.

We were proud to be the first NFC team in history to win fourteen games in a season, and for the second straight year we had the best record in all the NFL. Mark Moseley set an NFL kick scoring record with 161 points for the season and was also high scorer overall. Riggins was second with 144, making it the first time since 1951 that the top two scorers had played on the same team. Their combined total of 305 points was higher than the total scores of eight other NFL *teams.*

In the play-offs, we would host the Rams while the Forty-Niners (10–6) played the Lions (9–7). In the American Conference, Miami (12–2) would play Seattle, while the Raiders (12–4) played Pittsburgh (10–6). We were the defending champions and the favorites. We had the home field advantage, and we couldn't wait for New Year's.

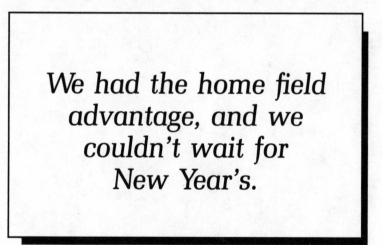

We had the home field advantage, and we couldn't wait for New Year's.

Back to the Super Bowl

We had scored 541 points during the regular season, by far the most in the history of the club. We were eager to show off our offense in the play-offs, but we didn't take the Rams lightly. Though we had beat them convincingly five weeks before, running up a 42–6 lead and winning 42–20 at their place, this was the play-offs and anything could happen. Teams that have had rough years can turn things up a notch in the post-season and surprise the favorites.

We must have been so worried about that that we over-achieved. We built a 24–0 lead and allowed the Rams just one touchdown. We led at the half 38–7 and won 51–7. John Riggins ran for 119 yards and scored three touchdowns, and Mark Moseley kicked three field goals. It was the biggest margin of victory in an NFL play-off game in twenty-six years and in the forty-seven-year history of the Redskins. We set or tied thirteen play-off records.

One more win and we would be on the way to our second Super Bowl. We knew that would require eleven straight victories since our one-point Monday night loss to the Packers, but by now we thought we could do anything. We were well aware that it was San Francisco coming to town, the ones who had handed us our fifth straight loss at the start of 1981. We hadn't played them since. They had gone on to win the Super Bowl that season.

No one knew as well as we did that the Forty-Niners

189

were a dangerous, powerful team with a quarterback, Joe Montana, who seemed to be able to perform the impossible. We didn't expect to blow them away. We simply wanted to do what we had been doing for weeks: building a big lead, making them play catch-up, and holding on.

It began almost according to plan. We held them scoreless early, but we were able to score only once in the second quarter. A 7–0 halftime lead was nothing to rest on. I felt better when we scored two touchdowns in the third period and still kept Montana and Co. out of the end zone. We moved into the fourth quarter leading 21–0, but the Forty-Niners were knocking. Theismann capped a 79-yard drive with a 5-yard touchdown pass to Mike Wilson twenty-three seconds into the period.

Five minutes later Montana beat the defense with a 76-yard first down touchdown bomb, and suddenly we had a football game. Two and a half minutes later, Montana did it again, leading the Forty-Niners 53 yards in four plays, the last a 12-yard pass to Wilson. In about eight minutes, leaving only seven minutes to play, we had maddeningly, frighteningly been caught by San Francisco.

Mark Moseley had missed four field goal attempts in the cold wind, but we knew he was our best shot at getting back on top. We took over on our own 22-yard line and worked at eating up the clock while trying to get into position to win.

This is where the home field advantage really pays off. If we had been in San Francisco and blown a 21–0 lead, their fans would have been going crazy and we might have felt overwhelmed by the dramatic change in momentum. But we were in Washington, and our fans had not given up. There was no stunned silence. They shrieked, *"Defense! Defense!"* when San Francisco had the ball, and when we took possession late, they were on their feet as one, screaming for a score.

Theismann led us 53 yards in six plays, and with forty seconds on the game clock, Moseley lined up for a 25-yard field goal. We knew that even if they blocked it or he missed, the game would still be tied. But San Francisco is a big play team. We had already had the ball eighteen more minutes than they had, yet they had gained more yards and were tied. We didn't want Montana to get the ball, even with a half minute left, and we certainly didn't want to go into overtime.

When that kick split the uprights, RFK Stadium was rocking. The Niners tried a couple of desperate passes, but the game was ours, 24–21. John Riggins kept his post-season rushing streak alive, running for 123 yards in 36 carries. We had won 11 straight and were heading to our second Super Bowl.

In the AFC Seattle had upset Miami 27–20 while the L.A. Raiders had beat Pittsburgh 38–10. The Raiders then beat Seattle 30–14 for the right to face us in the Super Bowl. We had beat the Raiders 37–35 in the fifth game of the season, so we knew they were explosive.

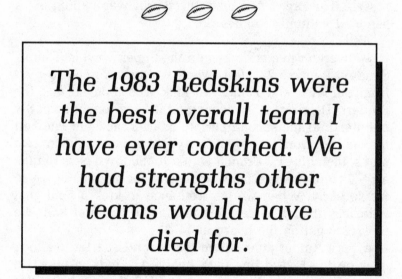

The 1983 Redskins were the best overall team I have ever coached. We had strengths other teams would have died for.

The 1983 Redskins were the best overall team I have ever coached. We had strengths other teams would have died for. John Riggins was the best fullback in football then, and Joe Theismann was as good a quarterback as any in the league. We were strong and deep at every other position, played great defense, and had special teams that covered like crazy. In sixteen regular season games and two play-off games, we had averaged 34 points a game.

Since I had become head coach in 1981, excluding the 0–5 start that year, the Redskins had lost two games in a row only once. My fantastic team was making me look good. In an article the day before the Super Bowl, the *Washington Post* called me a genius. I had been embarrassed when the press called me that before I had been hired—especially when Jack Kent Cooke had scowled over it. Now I tended to agree with them. Hey, how could I argue? Look at what I'd done.

Seriously, I knew better. I had been in coaching long enough to know how important a coach is and how crucial all the other elements are. The owner, organization, the team, health, everything goes into making or breaking a team. Sure, I was feeling good about the team and about myself. The press, the fans, the world was calling me a genius. I wanted to believe it.

Well . . .

We weren't five minutes into the Super Bowl in Tampa, Sunday, January 22, 1984, when we were forced to punt from our own end zone. The kick was blocked and the Raiders' Derrick Jensen recovered it for a touchdown. Six minutes into the second period, quarterback Jim Plunkett moved L.A. from their own thirty-five to our twelve in two plays, then hit Cliff Branch with a touchdown pass to take a 14–0 lead. It was a new experience for us to be down so far so early. When we got a chance to kick a field goal with less than four minutes to play in the first half, we took it to get on the board at 14–3.

After a Raider punt late in the second quarter, we took over on the 5-yard line with twelve seconds to play. Do you want to play Football Coach? What would you do? You make the call. You're down 14–3 against a team you have beat. This is the most important game of the year, and because it's now, it's the most important game in your life.

Do you fall on the ball and go into the locker room down by only 11? Or do you believe in the offense that got you where you are? Your team has averaged over 30 points a game, so you have the guys who can make it happen. No, you're not going to throw an 80-yard bomb, because even if your man catches it, it will eat up the clock. He'll be tackled deep and the half will be over. C'mon, you're the genius coach now, the confident one, the offensive strategist. You've got Joe Theismann standing there waiting for your instructions. Be decisive. Make a choice. Make something happen, or fall on the ball?

> *This is the most important game of the year, and because it's now, it's the most important game in your life.*

We were behind by more than a touchdown. We had time, I figured, for one screen pass to bust us out of there 25 or 30 yards and call a time-out. Theismann can loft one deep from there and we could pray for a miracle or at least have a chance of getting a pass interference call. It's our only hope of closing the gap by halftime. What did you call? I told Theismann, "Screen pass to Joe Washington! Nobody's gonna play man-to-man with us 95 yards away!" I wish it had been your call.

Theismann always tells the story with him shooting me three double takes and asking me four times if I'm sure I really want him to risk a short pass that close to our end zone. I don't remember it that way. I remember him being so gutsy and wanting so badly to win that he went back in there with fire in his eyes, determined to get us down the field with a short pass, a time-out, and a long pass.

He lined up over the center, took the snap, and danced back to set up. One linebacker, Jack Squirek, went right to Joe Washington, and Theismann threw the ball right into his hands. Interception, 5-yard run back, touchdown Raiders, end of half, Redskins down 21–3. The next day the *Washington Post* called me a buffoon.

Of course, I'm neither a genius nor a buffoon, but they were probably closer to the truth that day than they had been the day before. I had been doing the best I knew how all year long. When a risky play fails, it fails at the worst possible time. So, we all looked bad. But was I a different person from one week to the next? The press, the fans, the world is fickle. If I live by their standard I can go from a genius to a buffoon in two days. My life could be a roller coaster from week to week. I have value and am loved only if I make the right decisions and we win.

We were in a deep, deep hole, down by 18 at the half against the Raiders. We believed we could turn it around. We had supreme confidence in our ability on both sides of the ball. That day, we were wrong. The Raiders were monstrous on defense, holding Riggins to 64 in 26 carries. And their Marcus Allen, the great running back, ran for 191 yards in 20 attempts and scored two touchdowns, both in the third quarter. By then we had managed just one Riggins touchdown and our extra point attempt was blocked.

Our six points in the third had brought us to within twelve at 21–9, but Allen's 5-yard TD run made it 28–9, and a dramatic play at the end of the quarter all but put the game out of our reach. We never gave up, of course, but Allen ran for a touchdown all the way from the line of scrimmage on our 26 as time ran out in the third, and they took a 35–9 lead into the last period. They added a field goal as we sputtered.

It had been more than a year since we had scored fewer than twenty-one points in a game, and now we had been held to under ten in the biggest game of our lives. It hurt.

We had made some costly mistakes, and of course I was a buffoon. But we could take nothing from the Raiders. They had clearly been the best team that day.

Our loyal fans were smart enough not to judge our season by one tough loss. We'd had a regular season and play-offs before that which had resulted in sixteen wins and two one-point losses. We received a warm welcome back to Washington, and we were eager to enjoy time away from football.

New Eyes

I have always been happy that I can provide things for my kids that I might not have been able to if I had not become a pro coach. I don't want them to get the impression that things are handed to you in life. They are expected to work and to contribute. But it was a thrill to me to be able to offer J.D. a nice car when he was old enough to drive, provided he maintained certain grades. Had he expected it or demanded it or proved unworthy of such a gift, I would have yanked it back. But this was a good kid, responsible, hard working. It's true he needed that incentive for his school work, and it was effective.

He would turn sixteen in February of 1985, and I'll never forget shopping with him for a Camaro several weeks before that. We sat in the little bucket seats, and I could see in his eyes how much he loved that car. The salesman very helpfully pointed out to me—in front of J.D., naturally—that for just a thousand more, we could "move into" not just a Camaro, but a Z-28.

I was in a mood and on a roll, and you can imagine the kind of encouragement and promises I was getting from J.D., not to mention from the salesman. We ordered the Z-28, and J.D. selected all the colors and options. He was almost as happy about it as I was. Maybe it was a mistake, maybe I shouldn't have done it, but it was one of the most gratifying experiences of my life. This wasn't trying to please a spoiled kid. This was being able to give my son something I could never have had. If I thought it would be bad for him, I wouldn't have done it. I was grateful to have the means—especially now with the real estate deal—and I was doing for my son what I know my dad would have done for me if he could.

I don't know how J.D. stood the wait for that car. It would be several weeks before we could expect a call from the dealership.

We'd had a tough year, and not just on the football field. The previous summer, while still lamenting our tough Super Bowl loss and yet enjoying the admiration of the city that had seen two straight Super Bowl appearances, I began getting troublesome mail. Late notices. Some of my mortgages were not being paid on time.

The first couple of notices were just nuisances. I hardly gave them a second thought. I called my partner and sent them to him. He would take care of them. Just a bureaucratic blunder. No problem. Then more and more of them began to appear, and he became a little harder to get hold of. It made Pat nervous. To me it was just aggravation. I reminded my partner that I didn't expect or want this kind of hassle. That was his job. I provided the money. He was to handle the business.

Once, when I really needed some answers, he admitted that some of the units were not renting as we had hoped. People were moving out of the area. "Should we slow down?" I asked him. Not yet. It was too early to tell if this was just a slow phase in a fast growth. We wouldn't want to be caught with too few units when people were ready to rent and buy. Of course, by now I was only guessing. How could I know what to do during a market downturn?

The season was approaching, and I had to stay out of it, even though I didn't like the news from my real estate development. The economy was failing. Industries were closing. People were moving away. Hardly anyone was moving in. We were still building, still hoping, hedging our bets, hoping for a turnaround.

The mail became alarming. The partnership was not making its payments. I knew I had a problem, but I literally didn't have a minute to devote to it. I talked to my new friend Don Meredith, and he shared my anxiety. He advised me it was nothing to ignore. "I'm not a business man," I told him. "I'd like to have thought I was, but I'm just in this to turn a profit."

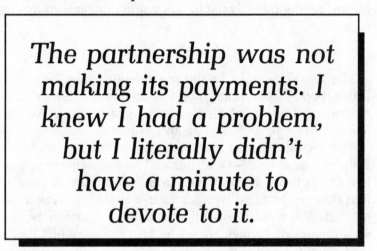

The partnership was not making its payments. I knew I had a problem, but I literally didn't have a minute to devote to it.

"Yeah, but you own these properties," he said. "The creditors are going to come after you."

"The partnership owns them," I said.

"You're a partner," he said.

I needed help. I asked Don if he would fly to the site and do some checking for me. I had a fear I wouldn't like what I heard. He came back with information so bad I could hardly understand it, let alone deal with it. I tried to bury the ominous feeling I had about my investments, but I couldn't.

Don had found a mess. The partnership had become a monster. The interest payments alone were nearly fifty thousand dollars a month, and that wasn't even counting the mortgages. I was about to start a football season. There was nothing I could do. I asked Don if he could go back out and try to handle it for me. "Help me, because I can't concern myself with this." Don went out there and hired three bookkeepers to try to get a handle on the magnitude of my problem.

During the season, I am immersed in football. It commands almost every waking minute and I can be bothered with nothing else. There's no other way to function as a head coach in the NFL. The demands have shortened the careers of many coaches. I trusted Don to handle things for me on the business side so I could concentrate on the game.

The Redskins split in the pre-season again, ironically losing both of our home games—one to the Super Bowl defending Raiders, of all teams, by just a point. We also lost a close one to New England at home.

The regular season had begun on a downer when the Dolphins beat us 35–17 at home. The following week we lost by six to the Forty-Niners in San Francisco. It was the first time we had lost two games in a row since November of 1981. We would win all of our next fourteen regular season games, enough to get us into the play-offs, but it was a tough year.

After those two opening losses we had won five straight (against the Giants, the Patriots, the Eagles, the Colts, and the Cowboys). Then we lost a pair of road games to the Cards and the Falcons and quickly fell from 5–2 to 5–4. We then won six of our last seven, including the last four, to finish 11–5. In the final two games we had beaten the Cowboys by two on the road and the Cardinals by two at home.

While we were busy earning the home field advantage for the first round of the play-offs, I put out of my mind what was happening with my investment. In many ways, I really didn't want to know. I had to concentrate on the Bears and the December 30 play-off opener. I didn't know it would also be our play-off closer. The Bears brought a 10–6 record to the game at RFK and beat us 23–19. They

were a year away from a 15–1 regular season, two shut-
outs (including one over us) in the play-offs, and a huge
win over New England in the Super Bowl. In 1984, however, they beat us, got shut out by the Forty-Niners, and
saw San Francisco run away with everything.

I would have liked to see us go farther, but I couldn't
complain about our 11–5 record, especially after dropping
the first two. I was excited about our personnel and our
system, but our season had ended too early.

I couldn't ignore Don and his bad news any longer. He
had spent sixty-four days near my properties over a six-
week period, with bookkeepers going over every check
and transaction. He uncovered a complex deal that had
depended on an industry boom that went bust. When the
mortgage payments were due, the partnership borrowed
from one fund to pay off another. Finally the funds were
depleted, the bills overdue, and the thing was crumbling.
The bottom line was, I had been a fool. I owned real estate I could no longer pay for. I couldn't even keep up with
the interest payments. The apartments were not renting,
and the buildings certainly would not sell.

Two weeks after the loss to Chicago in the play-offs I
spent the day with Don in the city where my money was
fast evaporating. I had hoped and prayed that he was
wrong, that something would turn, that it wasn't as bad as
I thought it was. In truth, it was worse. I was going deeper
into debt every day. Not only had I lost every dime I'd put
into the thing, but also my obligations were piling up, com-
pounding every day.

I worried most about this becoming public knowledge. I
was the partner easiest to contact; my name was on all
the documents. Just one nosy or noisy clerk could have
blown the whistle on me, and I would have been on the
covers of the news and sports magazines. I would have
embarrassed myself and my family, my owner, my ball
club, even the city of Washington.

Foreclosure notices had come to our home. Pat had sat
crying over the scary mail. Notices were filed, warnings

sent. It was a horrible time for her, and I felt the worst
about that. She had known. She had tried to warn me. But
I knew better. Rather than putting my faith and trust in
God, I had put my faith in myself and the almighty dollar.

When I got out there with Don and spent all day and all
evening realizing the magnitude, it hit me. Whether I ever
filed officially or not, I was bankrupt. I was through. I was
in way over my head, and I couldn't see the surface. I was
drowning in a sea of debt. That is a panicky feeling you
can't know or understand unless you've been through it.
It's as if your whole foundation has been torn out from
under you. You no longer believe in yourself. It's a night-
mare.

I couldn't believe it. How could this have happened?
My whole point was to get into something I didn't have to
think or worry about.

My contract had been renegotiated and I was in the
quarter of a million dollar a year range, but that looked
minuscule compared to these debts. I wondered what
would happen to my home, my family, my future. I called
Pat to tell her the awful news. We were deep, deep in
debt.

She didn't berate me or say I told you so. In fact, she
said, "You're going to kill yourself trying to put all this
back together. You got used and taken. There was nothing
you could do about it. Just file bankruptcy and come on
home."

I knelt by the bed in my hotel room and wept as I
prayed. I admitted to God that I had been a fool. I knew I
had depended on my own smarts to give me financial security. I had not trusted Him for my future. I had given
Him a lot of lip service while I was trying to stockpile my
fortune. Now I was at rock bottom with no one to
trust but Him. I was finally in total dependence on the
Lord.

I sensed He didn't want me to file bankruptcy. I had
gotten myself into this mess, and I would have to seek His
help to get me out. It wasn't fair to my creditors to make

them lose money. I finally reached a level of peace about my situation. I wanted all the help I could get, and I would get advisers and a lawyer and we would get to the bottom of the mess and start digging our way out. If it took me years, I would do it.

Once I had come clean and seen myself for what I was, God lifted me up. The peace He gave me about it didn't make it easier. And over the next several months, when I found that even the experts hardly understood all the complications, the financial failure became an ordeal like few I've gone through. I did believe there was a purpose even in that, just as there always is in any trial. It sure has changed the way I look at money and security. I believe I have finally learned to listen to my wife too. Never again in my life will I give someone the power to use my name without my approval.

While we worked and studied and tried to piece together the maze the investments had created, new bills would pop up. We'd think we finally had it under control, finally knew the scope of it and had decided on a long range plan to start chipping away at it, and news would come of more bills. I had loans and payments and bills I hadn't even been aware of. Things were charged to my account that I had never heard of.

During all of that, I had a peace about God's working in my life. I believed He still loved me, even in my stupidity. He had allowed me to fail in a big way, but because I had decided to honor Him by not taking people down with me. He gave me a confidence that He would not forsake me.

If I hadn't belonged to Him and hadn't known that for sure, I would have gone haywire over a deal like this. Humanly speaking, there was no way out. And the potential for it going public terrified me. But I told God I was even ready to go through that if that's what He wanted. "You're the only One who can handle this, the only One who can straighten it out."

Eight banks were involved in that town. When I had

finished praying and crying, I found Don. "I'm going to face every one of these bankers and be truthful with them," I said, "I'll tell them exactly what happened and exactly where I am, and we'll see if we can work something out for me to pay this down over the long haul."

"Mom," he said, "tell Dad I don't need that car."

I was liable for everything that partnership had done, whether I had been there or signed my name or not. That was the biggest lesson I learned on a human scale. Spiritually, I finally learned to put my entire trust and faith in God for my future and for my security. There's nothing wrong with investments and trying to make money, but there are ways to do it and ways not to do it, and I had sure learned that the hard way. From that point on, every deal would be prayed about and talked over with Pat. But that was almost funny now. It would be years before we had extra money to even think about. All my excess cash would go into extended term bail-out loans for a long time.

While I was working with Don at the site, I called Pat one night and found her in tears. She told me she had been resting on the couch in front of the TV and J.D. thought she was asleep. She overheard him praying, "Help Dad out there with this real estate thing."

When he noticed later that she was awake, he came and sat beside her.

"Mom," he said, "tell Dad I don't need that car."

That tore my guts out. That kid cared about me and loved me enough to offer to give up a car like that. I'll tell you what, if I'd had to sell my house and lose my job and dig ditches or wash dishes, I wouldn't have canceled the order for that car.

Picking Up
the Pieces

Don Meredith put me in touch with Robert Fraley, a young Orlando attorney who represents players and other athletes, as well as several NFL coaches. I had heard of him from a friend in the NFL and have since been involved with Robert on a number of projects. But one of the most important things Robert ever did for me was to help me see my way out of the financial mess.

It wasn't easy. He brought in the best experts to study it and to advise me, and that was complicated by the surprise notices that kept coming. Sometimes weeks and months later we would get another bill that would throw the solution out of whack.

I appreciated all the help and would develop some new and wonderful friendships through this experience, but the hardest part of the job—paying my way out—fell to me, and rightfully so. There was no way I was going to find a million dollars anywhere fast, so my goal was to get out of the real estate whatever it was worth. I wanted to find out what the unhappy totals were and start paying them down.

God had given me little warning signals, like the racquetball and other fiascoes, but I hadn't listened or noticed. Now He had my full attention. I had not followed His precepts in getting into this, but I was sure going to follow them in getting out of it. Only God could have worked this mess out.

A friend of mine from my boys' home board, Jerry Campbell of Texas, asked if I would visit him so he could see if he could be of any help. Don and I flew to Dallas right away. We hadn't been off the plane for an hour before Jerry and a friend of his I had never met took us to a bank and co-signed a loan for $125,000. I was stunned. This was the love of Christ.

With that check in my pocket, Jerry asked Don and me to come with him to see a professional sports team owner, a man I had heard of but had never met.

After the pleasantries, Jerry said, "Joe, why don't you tell him what has happened to you?"

The team owner sat forward as if me and my story were the only things important to him just then. I began to tell him about how I had thought I needed a secure investment and how I was sure I had found it. I got about halfway into the story and he stopped me.

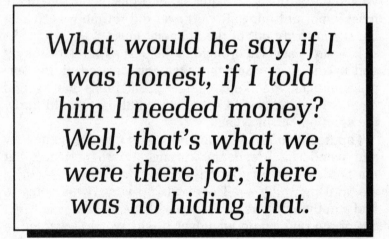

What would he say if I was honest, if I told him I needed money? Well, that's what we were there for, there was no hiding that.

"Joe, you don't need to tell me any more. Don't say anything else, because I don't need to know. Just tell me what you need."

I didn't know if I had bored him or what. What would he say if I was honest, if I told him I needed money? Well, that's what we were there for, there was no hiding that.

"I'd like to borrow some money," I said softly.

"Tell you what," he said quickly. "I'll lend you two hundred thousand." He went to the bank and signed for it that day. I left Dallas with $325,000 in loans from people I had just met. That was the first miracle.

My head was swimming by the time I got back to the banks in the city where I had the real estate holdings. I did not deserve this. What I deserved was bankruptcy. Sometimes, I guess, God lets us go as far down as we can go on our own before we fully trust Him. Then and only then He shows us what He can do. I had quickly gone from an overconfident real estate tycoon to a humbled, humiliated failure.

We went back and started visiting in person the banks involved. At the first one I discovered that the partnership had obligated me to three different loans on several properties totaling $1.58 million. When we finally found the right person to talk to, I was honest and open to the point of bluntness.

"I don't have the money, but I'm open to working out something with you so I can pay you off down the road. I'm not going to file for bankruptcy if you can work with me."

The man studied the documents and said he had to meet with other people and would get back to us. By the end of the next day he had a proposal. I held my breath. I was sure they would try to stretch out my payments over a long period, maybe like one huge thirty-year mortgage, but I didn't even want to think what the payments would be on $1.2 million. I had more than that again tied up elsewhere.

"We take the properties," he said. I nodded vigorously. I had little idea what they were worth, but they weren't worth much to me. I wanted out from under them. "All of them. The buildings, the lots, everything." I nodded again. "You purchase a $95,000 zero coupon bond that pays dividends to us for seven years."

"Uh-huh," I said, waiting for the other shoe to drop.

He sat staring at us. "Does that sound manageable?"

"Yeah," I said, still assuming it was some sort of a minimum first step.

"That's satisfactory then?" he said, sliding a form across the desk for me to sign.

"What are you saying?" I said, my heart beginning to race. I mean, I had prayed about this, but this was ridiculous.

"You turn over to the bank the properties and everything associated with them, free and clear. You give us a check for $95,000, which we will invest in zero coupon bonds, dividends payable to us for seven years."

"And that's it?"

"Do we have a deal?"

I tried to keep from grinning. This was a joke, right? He was kidding, huh, Don? Don wasn't smiling. I could see him trying to hide his excitement. I wanted to ask the man, "How can you do this? What's in it for the bank?" But I didn't want to risk the deal. He must have noticed my eagerness as I signed the papers. Without my asking, he explained.

"We're getting a fairly good deal on property that could one day be valuable again."

I wasn't about to argue. We shook hands and left, having turned then worthless real estate, which had me $1.2 million under, into a $95,000 dollar debt. We strode from that building with springs in our steps and waited to cross the street.

"What just happened in there?" I asked Don. "I don't understand this."

"I don't either," he said. "Keep walking."

I think ol' Don was worried the guy would come to his senses and come running after us.

That was the second miracle, and don't cringe at my calling it that. What would you have called it? I'll give you $95,000 for $1.2 million any day.

When I went to those eight banks with hat in hand, I wasn't pretending. There was no strutting, no cockiness, no defensiveness. I was scrambling, digging, fighting to pull together some deals with these banks. All I wanted them to know was that I was earnest and eager to keep from going into bankruptcy. I didn't want to rip anybody off, and I didn't want to leave anybody else holding the bag. Whatever my liability was, I wanted to take care of it, whatever it took.

Robert Fraley got personally involved and negotiated a deal where some of the banks would write off $879,000 in loans for two years' worth of interest ($160,000). The market was bad there, but people were hopeful it would return. They were betting the market would improve by the end of the two years.

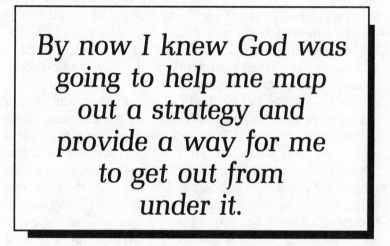

By now I knew God was going to help me map out a strategy and provide a way for me to get out from under it.

Nearly $2.5 million had been reduced to $255,000 in payments. There was still nearly a $1.5 million outstanding on houses and duplexes, and I was getting to the end of my resources. Now I had means I hadn't even known about a month before, so I was waiting to see what God would do. Despite the tremendous weight of the obligation and my chagrin over having caused this myself, I felt a certain peace. By now I knew God was going to help me map out a strategy and provide a way for me to get out from under it. It wouldn't disappear. These debts were not going away. But I was finding, or I should say God was providing, ways for me to live with them without my personal finances falling apart. My life-style might change, but somehow I would be able to handle this.

Still wondering where the last piece of the puzzle was going to come from, I headed back to Washington by way of Fayetteville to see George Tharel. I needed his counsel, his prayer, his encouragement. He was always behind me, no matter what.

🏈 🏈 🏈

For some reason, the Lord has often made it difficult for me to see George. I know He wants me to get with him, but it's on those side trips and detours that He often speaks loudest to me. This time I got a bad rental car. It had overheated once, and I had it patched up. When it began to overheat again, I was in the middle of nowhere and knew I could never make it all the way to see George if the car blew up on me again.

I had a choice. I could baby it and see how far I could get with the hood slightly open and the car crawling along in the night, or I could just stand on it and see how far it would go. You know me well enough by now to know what I did. I floored it and watched the temperature gauge max out. The little red lights flashed and then glowed solid. Smoke poured out of the car. I knew it was going to freeze up or blow up, one of the two, but at least the miles were whizzing past. I was taking a terrible risk. If it died out there, miles from anyone, I would have to spend the frigid night in that car at the side of the road.

Now it was desolate, eerie, lonely. I saw just a few tiny houses in the darkness. No service stations. There was a billboard for a small motel. Could I make it that far? Might they have a room? And didn't I have an old friend living around here somewhere? Yeah! There was that guy I had gone to high school with in California who had bought a couple of acres here and lived in a trailer on them while he was building his dream home. He had followed my career and had written once, inviting me to visit.

The car was making noise. I kept the pedal to the floor. When everything locked up, I would put it in neutral and see how close I could get to that little motel. Finally, inevitably, it happened. Everything shut down. I took my foot off the gas and let the car roll and roll and roll—right into the parking lot of the motel.

I signed in and, after calling the car rental company, I looked in the local phone book. Sure enough, there was the name of my old high school buddy. He'd been a heck of a football player. I called him. He was thrilled to hear from me and came and got me. When we got to his trailer I knew he had a story to tell, and I started to get a sense that this was another of God's plans. I thought I was supposed to see George—and I was; I spent a couple of days talking to him and praying with him—but God had planned this detour.

My friend and his wife were raising four kids in a trailer. He told me that the dream house had been only a dream for more than fifteen years now. He was not in my income bracket but his story was the same. What had done him in was an unwise loan of $16,000. How I wished that had been the extent of my problem, but I knew it was just as monumental to him as my millions' worth of debts were to me. That loan, which he had been unable to cover, had kept him from building his home all these years. He was paying it off slowly, just as I would have to do.

I realized that night that it was all relative. For young, single people, a five-hundred-dollar debt could change their lives. For some people, it might take ten million to hurt them. I was at my limit, and he was at his.

Most of us are going to be put through financial crises some time. That's why money is mentioned more than two thousand times in the Bible. The Bible gives us the blueprint for handling all our money: how to earn it, spend it, save it, invest it, give it, and teach our children about it. If I'd done more reading and studying than speculating, I might have learned that the Bible strongly discourages debt.

Money and security were weaknesses God had to deal with in my life. I want to pass along what happened to me so I can help keep my kids from falling into the same trap. You too.

◎   ◎   ◎

The question of what to do about the additional $1.4 million was answered after I had spent time with my friend and visited George. When I returned to my office in Washington I found a card on my desk from a local banker. By then I had seen all the bankers I cared to see in my life. Yet this nice little card, almost personal–like the ones preferred customers get–said, "If you ever need individual help for your banking needs, give me a call." And it was hand-signed. It was the type of a thing I might have tossed six months before. Now it hit me. Did a local banker really want to help? Would I be embarrassed to have him know how deep I was in debt?

I asked Don to talk to him confidentially and to tell him everything. "Tell him I need a hefty loan with a long-term payoff, and let him know I'm already under several other obligations."

Don did. The man listened and really cared. He said he thought his bank could see its way clear to help me in a significant way if I was willing to consolidate all my deals, everything we had worked out with all the other banks, and let him pay those off. Then everything would be in one place, one payment to one local account. No surprises, no list of different deals with varying interest rates and all that. To us it was yet another miracle. We were looking for a loan for the last big chunk, and we got a streamlined deal. It had a whopping price tag, of course, but no more than I would have had with all the separate deals I had floating around.

I pledged everything I had to that umbrella loan: my house, our summer home, my contract, insurance, all my assets, everything. All that stuff was hardly enough collateral, though my salary took a dramatic jump in July of 1985. My paychecks went directly into that account. With the new salary dollars and several new and newly-negotiated side projects engineered by Robert Fraley, I was able to come up with cash for the bail-out loan. For seven years most of my excess cash would go directly to those payments. It would be a long, hard, and very expensive lesson, but I learned it well. I would never have to go through it again, but I had needed it to wake me up.

Tough
Tasks

How can you really know who your friends are until they are tested? Don Meredith spent sixty-four days out of state for me and offered to lend me more money than he had. Other friends trusted me with money when my track record was terrible. I discovered friends I never knew I had.

I faced a huge problem that was insurmountable in human terms. I was bankrupt. I was gone. Yet through all of it I had friends stand for me, strangers come from out of nowhere, deals come together for little reason. It had to be God. There is no other explanation. And it was grace. I sure didn't deserve it.

The disaster had been another proof to me of the difference between the world and the people of God. The world would have laughed at me, ridiculed me, called me the buffoon and the fool that I was. But God stood by me, saved me from public embarrassment, and led me through this to other brothers and sisters in Christ. These weren't the people who tell you to go for it on fourth and one and then turn their backs on you when it fails. These were people who believed in me and showed me mercy.

When I look back on that horrible ordeal, I wouldn't trade it. I learned who my real friends were. I discovered my wife's steadiness and courage, and her forgiveness too. She was like a rock. She had not wanted us investing in the deal in the first place. She could have justifiably given me untold grief. I felt worse for her than for me. She's the one who really suffered. Yet her actions and her support said to me that even though I had flushed her immediate future, she was willing to stand by me, no matter what. How many men have wives like that?

One night, a couple of years into the experience, we went to see J.D. play football. He got beaten pretty badly, and that day we'd had more alarming mail about the real estate deal. It was a sad, gloomy time. That night, sitting on the bed, Pat turned to me and said, "Life isn't much fun right now."

I couldn't argue with that.

I believe that what I learned is a transferable lesson to anyone who has money problems at any level. Like I've said, if it's five hundred dollars, to you that may seem insurmountable. Other people would love to have had *only* the extent of my problems. Regardless, if the numbers are way past your range and you don't know how you got into the mess, let alone how you're going to get out, it's time to turn it over to God. Be willing to do the right and honorable thing.

I can really blame no one but myself. I never had any intention of spending money I didn't have. I sure wound up doing that, but I spent years and years paying it back too.

Had I listened to my wife, I would be much better off today. What a waste! And yet what a lesson! I believe God had a purpose in it all and that I'm a better person for it.

Your weakness may not be money or security. Regardless what it is, if you believe in Christ and belong to God, He's going to continue working in your life until you whip it. Don't listen to the world. The world doesn't love you. They'll cheer you when you're on top, and they'll boo you on your way down. God is the only One who loves you, and if you're like me, you'll understand this more during the bad times than during the good.

> # When I quit listening to the world's myths about success and happiness and left in God's hand the job of promoting me to a head coaching job, He did it.

When I quit listening to the world's myths about success and happiness and left in God's hand the job of promoting me to a head coaching job, he did it. When I quit listening to the world's myths about money and things and learned the hard way to trust only in God for my future, He bailed me out and helped me start over.

Like anyone else I had wanted to be happy and successful, and that was the path I had been on since college. I took the long road, but I discovered that what I was looking for was not something to be pursued. Success and happiness were by-products of a life given over to God. It seems I had to learn that lesson more than once, and in many ways I'm still learning it.

🏈 🏈 🏈

Despite living under the gun, having most of my money tied up in trying to lower my debt, I felt relieved going into the next football season. The system was in place to keep me from bankruptcy. I couldn't have any shopping sprees, of course, but our standard of living wasn't noticeably different. I was a blessed guy, and I still had a great, fun, and otherwise lucrative job.

We had a decent 1985 season. Most teams feel that 10

wins is a good goal. Maybe if we hadn't won 12, 16, and 11 the three previous years, we would have agreed. The biggest problem with going 10–6 in 1985 was that it didn't even get us into the play-offs. The Bears shut out the Giants and the Rams in the play-offs and took their 17–1 overall record into a Super Bowl mismatch against the Patriots. The Bears won 46–10.

It had been one of those years for us. We had won all four pre-season games (the first three by five points or fewer). Then we had lost the regular season opener big at Dallas, 44–14. We beat the Oilers close at home, 16–13, then dropped the next two (19–6 at home against the Eagles and 45–10 to the Bears in Chicago). So we were 1–3 and suffering. We then won a pair of home games and two of three on the road to take four of five and run our record to 5–4. We lost by six to the Cowboys at home, then beat the Giants and Steelers to go to 7–5. After a big loss to the Forty-Niners at home (35–8), we were 7–6 with three games to go.

Three straight victories let us close out with a 10–6 record, but it was no fluke turnaround. We had been struggling through one of those kinds of years you hate, where you just can't get untracked. We lost two in a row just once, but those three straight wins at the end made up our longest victory streak too.

That marked the third year we had won at least ten regular season games, and thirty-five regular season wins was also a club record for a three-year period. But the sad fact was, we had not looked very good, especially early. The fans and the press were on Joe Theismann's case, believing he had lost something in his game. I was so close to him, so identified with him, that it was hard for me to recognize. It's true, we weren't jelling. We had been 5–5 going into a big home game against the Giants, and we were under siege.

I was defensive of Joe. It was as if all those years and all those gutsy plays and all that loyalty and productivity had made him part of me. I could see through his eyes. The bad passes and the blown plays were not his fault, he and I thought. We really believed that. There was a bad break, a hand in his face, a letdown in the blocking, the sun in his eyes. For whatever reason, things weren't working, and he and I were taking the heat.

The problem is you don't just yank a starting quarterback, a Super Bowl quarterback, an all-pro, let's face it, a superstar. He was a veteran who had been to the top. Had he been a rookie or a young guy, I'd have moved him in and out, let him learn, disciplined him a little. But with an established thoroughbred, you coach a little differently. There's an ego to deal with, a guy's dignity. Our offensive production had dropped off dramatically, but you don't go pulling your number one quarterback when he's Joe Theismann.

Once you make a major quarterback change, that's usually it. You don't switch back. I kept thinking we were going to get back on track, so I wasn't ready to make a monumental change yet. Fate made the decision for me.

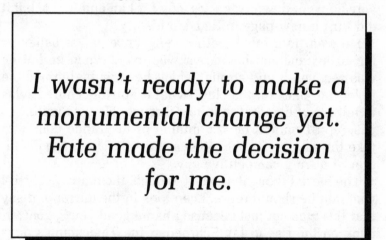

I wasn't ready to make a monumental change yet. Fate made the decision for me.

We trailed the Giants and were in danger of slipping under the .500 mark late in the season on Monday Night Football. Joe was sacked and had his leg broken so severely that millions on national television could see the bone sticking through the skin and even through his sock. Few, except Joe himself, expected him to ever come back.

It was a horrible injury and a serious blow to Joe and to our team. Sometimes you can't avoid gallows humor at times like that. He seemed to be handling it okay before being carried from the field, so I said, "Well, this is a fine mess you've left me in!" He laughed, as much as a man can when his leg had been shattered.

Ironically, Joe's backup, Jay Schroeder, came on and brought us back to a 23–21 win over the Giants. Joe went down with seven completions in ten attempts for 50 yards and one touchdown. In just part of a game, Schroeder was 13 for 20 and 221 yards, including a TD pass. It was the first of five wins in our last six games, and we would start the next season winning our first five and eleven of our first thirteen.

I'll never take anything away from Joe Theismann and the great years he contributed to our football team. The way he went down was a tragedy for him and for us, but it did turn a new page in Redskin history.

He went into rehab with a vengeance, never believing for an instant that his career was over. When he felt he was recovered and strong, which he was, he lobbied me to let him back on the club. What a horrible chore it was to tell a guy like that that he's through. He was willing to pass up $1 million or $1.5 million of insurance money to take the salary of a backup quarterback. That's the definition of a truly competitive guy.

The more I thought about it, though, the more resolved I was that he should retire. I can look in the mirror and say that this was not just because I had a good young quarterback on the rise in Jay Schroeder. Joe Theismann's days were over. He could have played. He could have competed. He might have even excelled. But the bottom line was that it didn't make sense.

I said, "Joe, you've been to the mountain. You've been one of the great players of the game. You've got a Super Bowl ring. You've gone to the Pro Bowl. You've done it all. You've hurt yourself badly, and I've got serious doubts whether you can come back and run around and do all the things you used to do."

"I can do it, Coach. I know I can. You know I can."

"Joe," I said, "why do this? What are we talking about? You returning to be a backup? It's ridiculous. I don't think I could look at you and feel comfortable about that."

He was like a champion racehorse. If he'd come up lame on the track, we'd have had to put him to sleep to keep him from running. I knew where his heart was. He had always believed he was the best, and he believed it still.

"Joe," I added, "even if you did come back, we're talking about probably one more year, risking worse injury. What for? Why risk not being able to walk when you're through with the game? You'd trade that for one more year?"

"I'm convinced I can play," he said. "I'm willing to forego everything, no matter what it takes."

"I know you are," I said. "That's what made you the kind of a quarterback you were. But I can't do it, Joe. I think you need to retire. Go out on top."

He continued to disagree, but he could see I'd made up my mind. Maybe he thought I owed him more loyalty, but what kind of loyalty would it have been to unnecessarily risk his health? And maybe I had a better perspective than he did on his sense of self-worth. I knew what it would be like to see a guy like that roaming the sidelines with a jacket over his uniform, charting plays on a clipboard or hand signaling plays in from the coaches. No way.

"One thing I need to tell you, Coach," he said, "is that you should have come to see me in the hospital."

"You're right, Joe," I said. "That was a mistake. I couldn't come that night because it was so late we didn't get out of the stadium until two in the morning. You remember I called you every day."

"Yeah, and you told me you were busy getting the team ready."

"I was."

"But I was still part of that team, Coach. I needed you to come and see me."

"I know. That was no excuse, and I'm sorry."

I didn't know what else to say. I don't think he ever forgave me, and that has come out in some of his criticism as a broadcaster. But I know we're going to remain friends, and I still believe he was one of the best ever. He sure made us during the early 1980s.

Now we looked forward to the 1986 season, the fiftieth in the history of the Washington Redskins. The first coach, Ray Flaherty, came to a rally the day before our regular season opener to help kick off the season.

In the pre-season we had dropped our first game and then won three straight. We had a roster full of new faces, fifteen of them. It was time to shake things up and get moving with the new quarterback, Jay Schroeder. I had the feeling that we had the makings of a great team. We had finished the previous season impressively and had a good pre-season. How good were we? Only the regular season would tell. We'd start with a pair of home games, and then we would visit my former employers, the San Diego Chargers, for a game I still remember.

Comeback!

My first year with the Redskins, 1981, we had scored 347 points in the regular season, two fewer than our opponents. It made sense that we finished even at 8–8. The next season we played just nine regular season games and outscored our opponents 190–128 to go 8–1. In 1983 we scored 541 points to our opponents' 332 in a full sixteen-game season (we were 14–2), and then we started to drift.

Our 11–5 season in 1984 saw us outscore our opponents 426–310, and the following year we were 10–6 and were outscored 312–297. Most encouraging, had been our turnaround at the end, when we won five of our last six.

In the 1986 pre-season we dropped our first game and won the last three, averaging nearly twenty-six points in the victories. Then we were off to the races. John Riggins was gone, and our new backfield workhorse was George Rogers out of South Carolina. He had come on strong in his rookie season in 1985. In our last three victories alone, he had run for 150 yards on 36 carries, 95 yards on 24 carries, and 206 yards in 34 carries (a club record).

The way to succeed in the NFL is to put together winning streaks. That may seem an understatement, but to get into double digit wins for a season, you've got to avoid those pairs of losses. We would not lose two in a row in 1986 until very late in the season, and we started with five straight wins.

We beat the Eagles 41–14 at home on opening day, and Rogers ran for 104 yards. He added 80 the next week when we hosted the Raiders, the team that had beat us in the Super Bowl following the 1983 season. Except for a one-point loss to them the following pre-season, we had not played them since that Super Bowl. This time we won 10–6.

On September 21, 1986, we traveled to San Diego and fell behind the Chargers by 18 points at the half. With the best comeback in my years as a coach, the Redskins stormed back in the second half. We needed a touchdown to win in the final two minutes, and Schroeder hit back-to-back passes to wide receiver Gary Clark for the 69 yards we needed. We won 30–27, though the Chargers had possession of the ball a full five minutes longer.

Rogers had run for 87 yards. While Charger Dan Fouts and our Jay Schroeder had each thrown the ball thirty-six times, Fouts had twenty-two completions for 235 yards and a touchdown (plus three interceptions), and Schroeder had sixteen completions for 341 yards and a TD (no interceptions).

We finished September perfect at 4–0 with a 19–14 win over the Seahawks (Rogers ran for 115 yards). Our fifth straight win came at New Orleans, 14–6, with Rogers running for 110 yards. Our first loss came October 12 in Dallas where the Cowboys stopped both our passing and our running game and beat us 30–6. As I've always said, the test of a good team is how it responds to a tough loss. We came back with a 28–21 win over the Cardinals at home (Rogers ran for 118 yards) and took a 6–1 record into New Jersey to face the Giants.

Somehow we seem to rise to the occasion for those Monday Night Football games. Even when we don't win, like when we lost to the Packers 48–47 in October of 1983, we usually put on a show. While George Rogers was held to 30 yards rushing, Jay Schroeder completed twenty-two of forty passes for 420 yards in a 27–20 loss. His main target was Gary Clark, who broke Art Monk's single game club receiving record with 241 yards on eleven receptions.

That was a tough game to lose, but we were still 6–2 and three of our next four games were at home. We had developed some great football players in Schroeder, Clark, Rogers, rookie Kelvin Bryant, and of course our veteran superstars like Art Monk, Joe Jacoby, Russ Grimm, Dave Butz, Dexter Manley, and Jeff Bostic. I hate to single out names because we had so many outstanding players, but you can see why we were optimistic about the rest of the schedule.

November was another perfect month for us. We beat the Vikings 44–38 at home in overtime, the Packers 16–7 on the road, the Forty-Niners 14–6 at home, the Cowboys 41–14 at home, and the Cardinals 20–17 away. Avenging that first Cowboy loss was sure satisfying. We outscored them 34–0 in the first two quarters, the most points they had ever given up in a single half. Our total points against them were the highest ever too.

The Viking game had been a barn burner. Rogers had run for 88 yards and Schroeder had passed for 378, but both were outshone by Tommy Kramer, the Minnesota quarterback. He had completed twenty of thirty-five passes for 490 yards!

Against Dallas, Schroeder had come through with a sixteen-pass, 325-yard performance to help carry us. Gary Clark caught eight passes for 152 yards.

Despite another 300-plus passing day for Schroeder on December 7, we lost to the Giants again, 24–14, this time at home. Kelvin Bryant had caught thirteen passes for 130 yards, but the Giants intercepted six of Schroeder's fifty-one passes and neither team gained even 100 yards on the ground.

Next came our second loss in a row, a 31–30 edging at Denver. A little turnaround somewhere in that game would have given us a 12–3 record, but we fell to 11–4. We finished with a 21–14 win over the Eagles at their place. We were 12–4, had outscored our opponents 368–296, and had the home field advantage for the opening round of the play-offs against the Rams. If we got past them, we would face the defending champion Bears in Chicago.

After that we assumed we'd face our nemesis that year:
the frustrating Giants who had already beaten us twice.

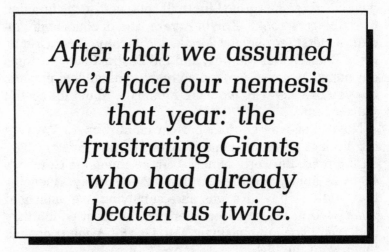

After that we assumed we'd face our nemesis that year: the frustrating Giants who had already beaten us twice.

I wasn't paying much attention to it, because to me it seemed like the accomplishment belonged to the entire coaching staff, but the press and our public relations people were making a big deal out of my being tied with George Allen for most overall victories as a Redskin head coach—sixty-nine.

Despite Eric Dickerson's 158 yards rushing (George Rogers had 115), we beat the Rams 19–7 in the first round and my coaches and I had our seventieth overall win. We had a good team and had had a great year. We wanted to make it to the divisional championship game for the third time in five years, and we didn't want to stop until we made the Super Bowl again.

On January 3, 1987, we faced the Bears in Chicago. They were the defending Super Bowl champions and one of the greatest teams ever. They had finished atop the NFC Central with a 14–2 record, and though they were down to their third quarterback, nobody gave us a chance. They were the odds-on favorites to win the whole thing again. In one of the biggest upsets of my coaching career, we held Walter Payton to 38 yards on fourteen carries,

Schroeder hit Monk with two TD passes, and we won 27–13.

As we expected, the Giants (14–2) had advanced by whipping San Francisco (10–5–1), 49–3. We hoped our third meeting with them that season would be the charm. It wasn't.

In a game that clearly showed their superiority, especially on defense, they shut us out 17–0. The Giants would go on to beat the Broncos 39–20 in the Super Bowl.

You'd think we would have been satisfied with a 14–5 overall record for a season, but we weren't. The Giants had beat us three times and won the Super Bowl. So, clearly, we were only third best that year. It's almost easier to be tenth than second. Second means you just didn't quite have what it took to get over the top. That, as has so often been the case with me and my teams, was negative motivation. And negative motivation is sometimes the best.

Had we been 10–6 or so and had not been expected to beat anybody, let alone getting as far as we did, we could have been pleased. But to be that close, to believe we had the manpower and everything else it took to get to the Super Bowl, and then still not make it . . . that was hard. That worked on us during the off-season. We didn't want to come that close again and fail.

I think it made all the players work harder and stay in better shape. It made me more determined to be sure every detail was in place. To win it all, a team has to be obsessive about the fundamentals and the little things. I knew we had the talent, and the organization was built in such a way that it contributed to success.

In 1987 we would once again face a season in which the labor disputes would overshadow the games for a while. That had shortened the season in 1982 but didn't affect our success. Who could say what might happen this time? There were talks of walkouts and lockouts. I didn't like the idea, frankly, and I didn't think a strike would happen.

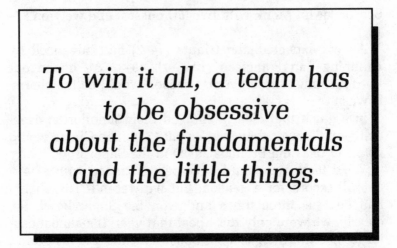

*To win it all, a team has
to be obsessive
about the fundamentals
and the little things.*

The pre-season got pushed back a week, but we quickly got on track, beating Pittsburgh 23–17 and shutting out Green Bay by 30. We then lost to Tampa Bay on the road and beat the Rams in Los Angeles for another 3–1 pre-season mark. By the time of the regular season opener, September 13, 1987, however, bad news was in the wind. The players and management seemed at an impasse. I didn't immerse myself in it or study it. I knew I was considered management, but all I cared about was that my team stayed together.

They tried to draw me into it, to get me to see their side, but I really didn't want to know all the details. I could probably be considered a traitor to management because I found the whole thing so distasteful that I tried to avoid it. You have to understand the obsession a coach has about team unity. Whatever else we brought into a game, whether it was personnel or strategy, overriding it all was team spirit, togetherness, an all-for-one-and-one-for-all mentality. If I knew anything about strikes, I knew that at some point some players were going to want to come back to work and some were going to want to stay out. Now what would that do to team spirit?

To be totally honest, when guys wanted to know what I thought, I didn't even talk about the issues. A guy has to decide what he has to decide and do what he has to do. If he feels the deal is not fair and not right, then he has to live with it or take action against it. I would not take a side.

But I did tell any player or group of players who wanted to know where I stood that I hoped they did whatever they were going to do *together.* Don't fragment yourselves. Don't choose up sides and start shooting at each other. Nothing but bad would come from that. I can truthfully say that I didn't care which side of the thing my guys came down on, as long as they agreed with each other. I'd like to think that maybe that forced them to think through and talk about the issues more than they might have otherwise.

I couldn't imagine skipping weeks of games or coaching a team of replacements.

Surprise

The season before, we had sent a club record seven players to the Pro Bowl. Russ Grimm and Joe Jacoby went for the fourth straight year, and were joined by Art Monk, Darrell Green, Gary Clark, Dexter Manley, and Jay Schroeder. They made up the nucleus of the team I thought had a good shot at winning it all that season.

We opened against the Eagles at home on September 13, 1987, and jumped out to a 10–0 lead. Jay Schroeder had started the game but was injured and had to be replaced by my old buddy Doug Williams. We had signed him during the off-season in 1986 when it appeared no one else wanted him. I thought he was a steal at about $400,000, a good, solid, veteran backup man. I knew him well, and he became a friend of Pat's too. I didn't know we would need him as our number one man in 1987's post-season. His performance would become one of the great chapters in Redskin history.

We had scored first against the Eagles on an early Jess Atkinson field goal, but Schroeder had missed on three pass attempts, then was injured on a 31-yard keeper. Doug replaced him and put us up 10–0 on a 6-yard TD pass to Art Monk. The Eagles tied us in the second, but we led 17–10 at the half and 24–10 early in the third.

The Eagles caught us again when Randall Cunningham scored on a 3-yard keeper, and then their defensive left end Reggie White recovered a fumble and ran it 70 yards for a touchdown. Time ran out on the third quarter with that play, and our Keith Griffin ran the ensuing kickoff back to their 39 to begin the fourth. Williams threw a scoring pass to Art Monk on the next play from scrimmage, and we never looked back. Williams had completed seventeen of twenty-seven passes for 272 yards and two touchdowns.

We were trying out kickers and gave punter Steve Cox a shot at a 40-yarder late in the game. He hit it to give us a 34–24 win, but we still needed a full time place kicking specialist. We found him in one of our old nemeses, Ali Haji-Sheikh. He would be with us just for that season, but what a season!

At Atlanta the next week we suffered a one-point loss on a missed extra point kick in the third period. Other than that one play we had traded the Falcons three touchdowns. It was a painful reminder of how important the little things are. I may be wrong, but I think part of our overall performance problem that day may have been the distraction of the strike talks. That and the Falcons' Gerald Riggs, who ran for 120 yards on twenty-three carries.

With that 21–20 loss we were 1–1 in the new season and primed for big things. I felt we had filled some important holes. Despite Haji-Sheikh's missed extra point and one blocked field goal, we believed we had found a solid kicker.

The experts who had predicted a player walkout following the second game of the season proved right. The National Football League Players Association struck the next day, and the games for the following weekend were canceled. The talks droned on, and neither side seemed willing to budge. The owners talked about bringing in substitute players, which bothered me. I didn't want to be involved in something that brought second-rate players across the picket lines and angered the veterans.

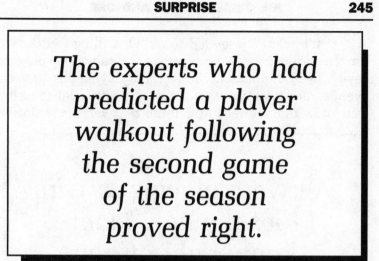

The experts who had predicted a player walkout following the second game of the season proved right.

I'm not going to try and kid you and say that the players who became Redskins for three weeks were just a notch below our first string teams. But I will tell you this: Those guys were great. They were fun to be around, and they were hungry. Most of them knew they would be gone when the strike was over. Only a few thought they really had a chance to hang on, but they all worked their tails off.

I was still concerned about my team, and I wanted them to stay together and come back together. Over the weeks of the strike, some teams split. Some players came back, making the competition uneven. We stuck with our substitutes, and it was a fantastic experience. I really got my mind changed, but not about the strike, and not even about making the veterans mad. What I learned was that when you put NFL hopefuls in NFL uniforms, work them out on NFL fields, and play them in NFL stadiums, they give you all they've got.

They weren't getting paid much. They knew it was temporary. But they had all played ball before, and at high levels. They weren't pretending or treating this as a lark. And I wasn't either. I still had a Super Bowl in mind, and if that meant taking a bunch of kids no one had ever heard of all the way to San Diego Stadium at the end of January

1988, that's what I intended to do. One thing I knew for
sure: Regardless how many games the substitute players
played, they all counted. We weren't playing just to keep
revenues flowing. We were playing to win. I let the new
team know right off the bat that this was serious business.

> ## We were playing to win. I let the new team know right off the bat that this was serious business.

One of the first things I noticed was that these guys
took advantage of the free food. Our regulars made
enough money that they usually ate out rather than filling
up on the burgers and sundaes provided for the players
the night before a game. There was always plenty of food,
and we coaches got all we wanted. With the replacement
players there, I didn't even get a burger! Those guys didn't
leave a thing.

They were hungry on the field too. After a short but
intensive training period, NFL games resumed the weekend of October 4, when we hosted St. Louis at RFK Stadium. Admittedly the crowd was down. We sold nearly
45,000 tickets but had 17,000 no shows. They missed a
good game.

We never trailed but we were tied at 7 and at 14 in the
third period. Then we pulled away to a 28–14 lead and
won 28–21. Our quarterback, Ed Rubbert out of Louisville,
completed fourteen passes for 334 yards and three touchdowns, all three to wide receiver Anthony Allen. Allen

caught passes totaling 225 yards, including one of 48 yards and another of 88 yards. With a whole new cast of characters, the Redskins were now 2–1.

Each week there was hope that the strike would end and that things would get back to normal. I hoped that myself, but meanwhile I was having the time of my life. These guys were playing their hearts out. The fan paying top dollar for professional football deserves the highest level of play possible, and no one will try to tell you this was it. But it was evenly matched and competitive, and these guys were no slouches.

Sunday, October 11, 1987, broke humid and rainy, and just over 9,000 fans watched us play the replacement Giants at East Rutherford, New Jersey. We broke a 3–3 tie in the second period with three straight touchdown runs, two by Wayne Wilson and one by Lionel Vital, who carried twenty-seven times for 128 yards. We scored in every quarter to rack up a 38–12 win. I wanted my regular team back, but I could sure live with winning. We were 3–1.

There were fewer than two hundred no-shows at Texas Stadium in Dallas the next Monday night, October 19. Several Cowboys had crossed the picket lines to return to the team, so the game looked like a true mismatch. On our side of the field we had names like Rubbert, Allen, Wilson, Caravello, Britz, Scissum, and Vital. On their side, along with several obscure names, were such established stars as wide receiver Mike Renfro, Danny White at quarterback, and Tony Dorsett at running back. On defense they had Ed "Too Tall" Jones and Randy White.

We gutted it out and somehow held them scoreless in the first half while we ran up a 10–0 lead. Midway through the third period they scored on a pass and came within three at 10–7. It was exhilarating to watch my new guys lay it on the line before a national TV audience. We added a field goal and held off the Cowboys for our third straight win, 13–7. Vital had outrun Dorsett 136 to 81, but Danny White picked apart our defense pretty well with twenty-one passes for 262 yards. Dorsett was held to no TDs and fumbled twice.

My regulars know me well enough to know what I think of them. I hated to see anything hurt them or their families or their futures. My excitement over coaching and winning with these young replacements says nothing about my feelings for the real Redskin team. I just have to say that it was fun and thrilling to be involved with these new guys for a while. I didn't like the strike, and I hated to see it. But I have a new appreciation for that second level of ball players, those guys who aren't at the NFL level in ability. They sure made up for it with desire, and I'll never forget the contribution they made to our 1987 season. By the time the strike was over and the real team came back, we were 4–1.

Jay Schroeder was also ready to resume as our starting quarterback. I was more confident than ever with Doug Williams as my backup, because he had shown he still had the skills and savvy to get the job done when we needed him.

The strike hurt us. We would eke out a few wins and deal with a lot of hard feelings before really getting back on track. Against the Jets at home in the first game back, we led 7–3 at the half but trailed 13–7 going into the fourth period. The Jets added a field goal, and with ten minutes to play, we were down 16–7. Schroeder capped a six play, 61-yard drive with a 2-yard pass to Kelvin Bryant, and Haji-Sheikh added the extra point to get us to within two at 16–14. Later Schroeder marched us 68 yards in nine plays and Haji-Sheikh hit a 28-yarder with less than a minute to play. Finally a one-point game had gone our way, 17–16. We were 5–1.

On November 1 we ran our record to 6–1 with a 27–7 victory over the Bills before more than 71,000 fans in Buffalo. We scored seventeen in the first half and ten in the third period to get out to a 27–0 lead. It was good to finally win something other than a nail biter. George Rogers had returned to form with 125 yards on thirty carries, and as a team we had gained 299 yards on the ground.

We thought we had things well in hand at Philadelphia the next week too, when we responded to their first touch-

down with three of our own. We had a 21–7 lead late in
the first half, but the Eagles weren't convinced. They
added a field goal and a Randall Cunningham to Mike
Quick TD pass before the half to draw to within four at
21–17. Neither team scored in the third, but the Eagles
took the lead 24–21 with the same TD pass combination in
the fourth.

We came back late on a 74-yard drive that ended with a
Schroeder to Gary Clark touchdown pass, but again we
couldn't hold the lead. Cunningham took the Eagles 77
yards in six plays and won the game with a 40-yard toss
to Gregg Garrity. By giving up two touchdowns in the last
quarter, we had lost 31–27. That was painful. We were
6–2.

We scored seventeen points in the second quarter and
went on to beat the Lions 20–13 at home the following
Sunday. Doug Williams saw a lot of action and would
start and play the entire next game against the Rams at
RFK.

The Rams beat us 30–26 in a frustrating game where we
could catch them only once. They jumped out to a 7–0
lead. We came back with a Williams to Monk pass, but
the kick failed so we trailed 7–6. Haji-Sheikh put us up 9–7
with a field goal, but they came back with a 95-yard Ron
Brown kickoff return that gave them a 14–9 first period
lead they never relinquished. We scored in every quarter,
but they stayed maddeningly out of reach.

Doug Williams had a great game for us, throwing for
more than 300 yards, including two touchdowns to Art
Monk. We were 7–3 and fighting to win our division and
make the play-offs.

Jay Schroeder came back against the Giants the next
Sunday, November 29. And I mean that literally. He completed twenty-eight passes for 331 yards and three touchdowns, all to different receivers, and they came late in the
game after we had fallen behind 19–3. We had been
shutout 16–0 in the first half, but with nine in the third and
fourteen in the fourth, we came from sixteen points down
to win 23–19 in the Washington rain.

We had to come from behind the next week in St. Louis too, but only because we had lost an early 10–0 lead. The Cardinals scored two touchdowns in the second to take a 14–10 halftime lead, and they scored first in the third period too, adding a field goal. We trailed 17–10 before breaking out with three touchdowns in the third on two runs and a pass. We won 34–17 and were 9–3. George Rogers had carried thirty times for 134 yards.

Rogers scored two touchdowns against the Cowboys on December 13, and Gary Clark caught 187 yards worth of passes, but we just barely won at home. We nearly had done to us by the Cowboys what we had done to the Chargers the season before and what we had done to the Giants just two weeks before. They say what goes around comes around. It almost happened to us.

Four of the first five scoring drives were ours as we built a 17–3 halftime lead and made it 24–3 in the third quarter. The last three scoring drives were the Cowboys' as, with a field goal and two Danny White TD passes, they drew to within four with three minutes to play. We won 24–20 in a game we never should have let get that close. Danny White had picked us apart with his twenty-seven completions to nine different receivers for 359 yards.

That should have prepared us for the great Dan Marino in Miami the next week when we put our 10–3 record on the line against the Dolphins. The problem is, there's only so much preparing you can do for a talent like that. It was a great game though, another of those where we traded scoring drives all the way and then looked at the scoreboard to see how it turned out.

Fast Finish

Nearly 66,000 were at Joe Robbie Stadium in Miami, December 20, 1987, for the fourteenth game of the season. Neither team scored until halfway through the second quarter when the Dolphins' Fuad Reveiz hit a 48-yard field goal. We traded touchdowns before the half, but their P.A.T. kick failed and we trailed just 9–7.

The rest of the way it was one touchdown at a time for each team. We led 14–9, trailed 16–14, led 21–16, and lost 23–21. Marino had led the Dolphins on two scoring 80-yard drives in the fourth quarter, both ending in passes to Mark Duper. They had hooked up three times in the game. Even though we controlled the ball for nine minutes longer, Marino's three touchdown passes and 393 yards passing had done us in.

Near the end of the game we let punter Steve Cox try a desperation 67-yard field goal, but it fell short. We were 10–4 with one game to play in the slightly shortened regular season.

We finished at the Hubert H. Humphrey Metrodome in Minneapolis the day after Christmas, 1987, in a game that would prove a perfect tune-up for the post-season. It might have been nice to cruise to an easy victory and be able to rest some people, but a tough, close one isn't bad heading into the play-offs either.

The Vikings took an early 7–0 lead, but we tied them in

the second quarter when our right corner back Barry Wil-
burn intercepted a pass at our goal line and ran it back
100 yards for a touchdown.

Jay Schroeder started at quarterback for us, but Doug
Williams soon replaced him because I thought we needed
a lift. Late in the third period Doug hit Ricky Sanders with
a 46-yard TD pass to put us up 14–7. The Vikings scored a
couple of seconds into the fourth on a 9-play, 80-yard
drive to tie it. Just five minutes later they had pulled away
to a ten-point lead with another touchdown and a field
goal. We had allowed them three straight unanswered
scoring drives.

With less than five minutes to play, Haji-Sheikh hit a
37-yard field goal, and three minutes later Williams hit
Sanders with a 51-yard scoring pass on third-and-one. We
went into overtime tied at twenty-four. Haji-Sheikh won it
27–24 for us a couple of minutes into the extra period with
a 26-yard kick on our first possession.

We were also most fortunate to have Doug Williams.
He was clearly the caliber of a starting quarterback,
which he had been for many years. As soon as the sportswriters realized he was going to be our starter throughout
the play-offs, they looked ahead to the Super Bowl. He
would be the first black quarterback to start in the big
game. Of course, they made a bigger deal out of that than
anyone else did, but it would be a proud moment for Doug
if we could get there.

Our first barrier were the Bears, who were just two seasons past their dominating Super Bowl season and are
always dangerous. They fielded pretty much the same
team, with stars like Walter Payton, Mike Singletary, Jim
McMahon, Dan Hampton, and Willie Gault. Like us, they
had gone 11–4 for the regular season, but they had the
home field advantage at frigid Soldier Field. The thermom-
eter said upper teens, but the wind chill was a minus
twenty-three.

San Francisco had won the western division and would
play Minnesota for the right to play the winner of our
game for the NFC championship. By midway through the

second period, that looked like the Bears. They had scored two quick touchdowns for the early 14–0 lead, and only a pair of Williams-led drives late in the second quarter caught them. George Rogers finished a seven play, 72-yard march with a 3-yard TD, and with just nine seconds remaining in the half, Williams hit Clint Didier with an 18-yard TD pass, finishing off a seven play, 69-yard drive. We felt fortunate to go into the locker room tied at fourteen.

Three minutes into the second half, Darrell Green electrified our team by running back a punt for a 52-yard go-ahead touchdown. Our guys held the Bears to a lone third quarter field goal and hung on for the 21–17 win. We really earned that one. Sanders caught six passes for 92 yards. Though Payton rushed for 85 yards, we kept him out of the end zone. We also intercepted three Jim McMahon passes.

Meanwhile, the Vikings had stunned the Forty-Niners, upsetting them 36–24. That gave us the home field advantage against the Vikes, which was a good thing after having just scraped by them in overtime two weeks before. They had beat the mighty Niners, and they believed they could beat us too.

> *They had beat the mighty Niners, and they believed they could beat us too.*

We played in our fourth NFC championship game in six years at RFK on Sunday, January 17, 1988, before nearly 56,000 fans. It was a hard fought, defense-dominated game. Late in the first period Williams took us from our own 2 yard line to the Viking 43 in seven plays, then hit Kelvin Bryant with a 43-yard touchdown pass. Neither team scored again until late in the second quarter when Minnesota quarterback Wade Wilson found flanker Leo Lewis with a 23-yard TD pass.

Haji-Sheikh broke the tie for us late in the third with a 28-yard field goal, but their Chuck Nelson matched that early in the fourth from 18 yards. Late in the game, Williams led us 63 yards in seven plays and then hit Gary Clark with a 7-yard scoring pass that proved to be the game winner. We became the first team in the 1980s to go to the Super Bowl three times.

In the AFC, Cleveland (12–4) had won the Central Division, Denver (10–4–1) the West, and Indianapolis (9–6) the East. Denver opened the play-offs with a 34–10 win over Houston while Cleveland beat Indianapolis 38–21. The Broncos then beat the Browns 38–33. It would be Denver's third trip (and second straight) to the Super Bowl. Their first had followed the 1977 season. They had lost in their previous appearances.

Denver was a misunderstood and under-appreciated team with a great quarterback and coach in John Elway and Dan Reeves. They had the reputation of not winning the big games, but that lie pretends that the Super Bowl is the only big game. We knew what it took to get to our three in the 1980s. Every post-season game is crucial. Denver had won a lot of big games.

Having lost the previous Super Bowl, they were a proud and dangerous team. They wanted to prove themselves to their fans and to the press. The game was played before 73,000 on a beautiful January 31, 1988, in San Diego.

We were forced to punt after our first possession and the Broncos took over on their own 46-yard line. On the first play from scrimmage, Elway connected with wide receiver Rickey Nattiel for a touchdown, and many believed the Broncos were on their way. Four minutes later they ran their lead to 10–0 on a 24-yard field goal after moving

37 yards in six plays and controlling the ball for more than two minutes. We went into the second quarter down 10–0.

That second quarter, however, may never be matched in Super Bowl history. We scored five touchdowns in five possessions, beginning with the first time Williams touched the ball in that period. He threw an 80-yard touchdown pass to Rickey Sanders. Our next time with the ball resulted in a 5-play, 64-yard drive that ended with a 27-yard pass to Clark. Running back Timmy Smith scored on a 58-yard run from scrimmage on the second play of our next possession. A few minutes later it was Williams to Sanders for 50 yards and another TD. Doug closed out our second quarter scoring with an 8-yard pass to Clint Didier.

> *It had been one of those devastating, game-turning periods of which you only want to be on the right side.*

It had been one of those devastating, game-turning periods of which you only want to be on the right side. We had come back from a ten-point deficit to pile up thirty-five points in the second period, and the game was as good as over. We added an early fourth quarter touchdown to win 42–10, breaking three Super Bowl records.

Doug Williams had completed eighteen passes for 340 yards and four touchdowns. Timmy Smith had the game of his career, carrying twenty-two times for 204 yards. Our offense had racked up more than 600 net yards and had controlled the ball for more than thirty-five minutes. We could not have asked for more from anyone. Doug Williams was named MVP of the game and would sign a multi-year deal at more than $1 million a year for us. Unfortunately for the Broncos, they would return to the Super Bowl again two years later to lose to San Francisco, 55–10. They joined the Vikings as the only teams who had been to the Super Bowl four times without a victory. In three of their four appearances they had scored just ten points. Like the Vikings, they proved to be one of the greatest teams ever, but have yet to win the Super Bowl.

San Francisco passed us up with two more Super Bowl appearances in the decade, winning both for four championships and rightful claim to the title: "The Team of the '80s."

Since that last Super Bowl experience, we have struggled to get back to top form. Doug Williams' back became a problem early in the 1988 season, so we brought in Mark Rypien out of Washington State. He has done a good job for us, but injuries have plagued us elsewhere too. I had my first losing season in Washington in 1988 when we lost five of our last six, including the last two, to fall from 6–4 to 7–9.

Williams had several good passing days for us, including a 30–29 win over the Steelers in the second game of the season. He completed thirty of fifty-two to nine different receivers for 430 yards and two touchdowns. When his back made it impossible for him to continue, we started Rypien against the Cardinals, who had moved to Phoenix. Though we lost 30–21, we liked what we saw at quarterback. Mark had a 300-yard passing day and three TD passes.

He threw for almost that many again the next week with 288 yards and two TDs in a heartbreaking one-point loss to the Giants, a loss that would characterize our frustrating season. We came back to win three straight over the Cowboys, the Cardinals, and the Packers, and at 5–3 we thought we were back on track. Rypien had another 300-yard game against Phoenix, but we came back with Williams for the win over the Packers.

A sort of unwritten rule in pro sports is that the starter doesn't lose his job because of an injury, no matter how impressive his replacement is. Doug led us to victory with twenty-five completions in forty-two throws for two touchdowns.

Williams and Rypien shared the duties in a big loss to the Oilers, and Doug came back with a 299-yard day in a close win over the Saints. He had another good day in a tough loss to the Forty-Niners, but we started Rypien against Cleveland the next week and lost a close one. They shared the quarterbacking duties until the last game when Williams played the entire game. Because of Doug's back problems, that would be his last appearance until November 5, 1989, when we started the second half of that season at 4–4 against the Cowboys at home.

Though he was 28 for 52 for 296 yards, we lost 13–3. We beat the Eagles the next week behind Doug, but now he was really ailing. Rypien took over as we started to gel, losing a close one to the Broncos to fall to 7–6, then winning our last five to finish 10–6 and just miss the play-offs. In a big win over the Chargers in the third to last game, Rypien completed twenty-three passes for 302 yards and two TDs. He threw for 290 yards in the season finale against the Seahawks. Doug had made his final appearance with a few plays in our win over Phoenix, December 3. It marked the end of a great career, and to my deep disappointment, it also ended a beautiful friendship.

Pain and Gain

For a team, and a coach, who had gotten used to going to the play-offs, missing it two years in a row was agony. The fans and the press had to wonder if we'd lost it, the team and I. There were those who felt we had grown complacent, that we were satisfied to play good football and collect our paychecks. I knew it wasn't true. My coaches knew it wasn't true. And most of all, the players knew. What people outside the game don't realize is how many things go into making a successful football team. It's no simple task.

I take responsibility for planning. We work hard to analyze every game and be ready for the next one. We push our team to stay in shape, to learn the offenses and defenses, to be able to work well with each other. We log the hours necessary to get that done whether we win or lose. The best I know to do is to put players on that field that are the top at each position in our organization. We provide a game plan and conditioning and motivation, and we see it through. Sometimes you lose because of bad breaks. Sometimes you lose because of mental or physical errors. Sometimes you lose because the other team is better than you are, either dominating you physically or taking advantage of good scouting and outthinking you.

You win games by scoring more points than the other guys, but you can lose in a whole lot of ways. One thing I have never been able to abide are people who think that a struggling football team doesn't care anymore. You can care too much, and that's what happens when you're pushing, overextending, trying to do more than you can do just to get back on top.

Something I like about Jack Kent Cooke is that I believe he has always understood that. He has never questioned our motives or our dedication. If and when we lose, it's certainly not because we have let down and quit trying. I expect peak performance from myself, my staff, and my players. Sometimes you lose anyway.

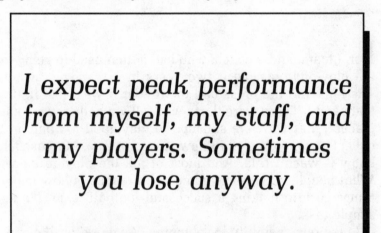

I expect peak performance from myself, my staff, and my players. Sometimes you lose anyway.

I never accept it. I pick a loss apart and can't wait till we face that team again. Even when they were clearly better and more well-coached, I dwell on it until I think I have it figured out. Maybe winning isn't everything *or* the only thing, but it sure is the object of the game. People like to tell you that what matters is how you play. I can't argue with that. What really matters is that you play to win– within the rules and as hard as you can go, all the way.

As I had to do with Joe Theismann, the day came when I had to have my chat with Doug Williams. Here was a proud, fiery man who had meant a lot to me and to our club. He had been a great star and achieved much. But he was getting too old, and his body had let him down. He was not the quarterback he had once been, and he would not be again. My resolve to be the guy who tells the veterans that their days are over was tested to the maximum in that conversation. Boy, I hated to do that.

If someone doesn't make the team as a rookie, I don't handle that. The player's individual coach gives him the bad news. If I had to do all of those every year I'd be so depressed by opening day that I wouldn't be able to function. But anyone who has made the team and has played for me, I feel like I owe it to him to tell him myself, face-to-face, in private.

Some of the hardest to tell were my favorite kinds of players. I hesitate to start listing them because there were so many. But guys like Pete Cronan (linebacker, 1981-85), Greg Williams (free safety, special teams, 1982-84), and Otis Wonsley (running back, special teams, 1981-85) were people I loved. They had great attitudes, were fun guys, and hit people like mad. Great character in all of them. They gave me everything they had, covered on kickoffs like nobody in the league, played hard on every down. If I'd known that telling guys like that that their careers are over was part of being a head coach, I might have thought twice.

Now it was time for the 1990 season, a new decade, a chance to become a contender, a play-off team again. And it was time for me to tell Doug Williams that our professional relationship was over. With input from people I trusted, I had made the decision.

First, he was hurt. He had a bad knee, and now he had also had major surgery on his back. For the past two seasons he missed as many games as he played because of injuries or operations. I didn't think he would be able to hold up as my number one quarterback.

Secondly, I had made the decision to go with two young quarterbacks. Mark Rypien was ready and Stan Humphries out of Northeast Louisiana was coming on. Yes, I needed a third guy, and preferably a veteran. I didn't see

Williams in that role. I was looking for a guy with his age
and even a lot of playing time, but not someone who had
tasted the Super Bowl. Doug had shone, had been a pio-
neer, had excelled, had won the MVP. Yes, I would go for
an older third QB, but I wasn't going to do that to Doug
Williams. For one thing, he would have to take about a
fifty percent cut in pay. I knew better than he did that he
would have a tough time with that.

I had had a preliminary discussion with him, hinting
that I wouldn't be able to keep him on the team at his
present salary. I didn't hear him say, "Hey, I'll take a cut."
He told me, "I'll tell you the truth, I earned that money. I
have the right to make that much." Maybe he did, but not
as a third QB.

I'm sure he would have taken the cut if he'd known that
would be the only way he could stay, but when I was
ready to talk to him I had already made up my mind. I
wanted to go after Jeff Rutledge of the Giants, another
veteran. I didn't even bring up the money with Doug.

Something else I didn't bring up—because it was too
late and I didn't want him promising to change just to
keep a job; he'd had his chances—was his conditioning.
As I look back on it, I should have mentioned it in that last
meeting, but I didn't want to rub it in and make Doug feel
bad. It's bad enough when you're through and you can't
talk your boss out of it. But I had wanted him to move to
Washington so we could keep better track of his conditioning. During a lot of the off-season he was home in
Louisiana. He could not work out the way he would have
if we'd had him in our own facility.

I had asked him several times in the past, and for short
periods he would stay around and work out. But it didn't
last. Was he the best trained guy on our football team? No.
If I had seen him on an exercycle every day during the off-
season when I went to the office early in the morning, or if
I had seen him on the practice field throwing everyday,
would it have made any difference? Yeah, it would have.
But you can't make a guy do something. If you have to

force a guy to work out, you're not going to get a good workout.

All those things went into a decision like that, and I've been grateful to be free to make my own decisions. I've made some personnel choices, activating a guy for the last week or two of the season, that cost Mr. Cooke tens of thousands of dollars. He trusts me to do what I think is right. What I thought was right in Doug Williams' case was to let him go.

I told him straight and as compassionately as I could. I didn't talk about the money, because it was no longer an issue. And I didn't bring up the conditioning because it was too late for that too. He wasn't happy. He argued with me. But I expected that. If he hadn't, I would have thought something was wrong with him.

I told him about my plan to go with the youth movement for my first two guys and to see if we could get Rutledge as a number three. I guess Doug doesn't remember that part of the conversation. I was as open and honest with him as I thought I could be, but later he was quoted in *Sports Illustrated* as calling me a liar. He says I told him he was too old for number three and then turned around and went with a veteran like Giant Jeff Rutledge.

Our friendship goes back a long way. I have always been sold on Doug, from the time I agreed with John Mc-Kay that Tampa Bay should draft him right up until the day I had to cut him. My hope is that Doug will not lay at my feet some of the unfairness that has dogged him for years. I still consider him my friend.

We took a big step toward getting back to where we wanted to be in 1990 by making the play-offs with a 10–6 record. We had to win five of our last seven to do that. We beat the favored Eagles, with whom we had split during the regular season, in the first round of the play-offs, then lost 28–10 in San Francisco to the defending champions. The Giants would beat Buffalo, a team we had beat in our finale, in the Super Bowl.

During the season we were 5–4 against play-off-bound teams, which made me optimistic about 1991. Mark Rypien had won thirteen of his last seventeen starts, but he missed six due to a knee injury. With him back and healthy, we're looking for another big year, a play-off season.

At the end of my tenth year in Washington our record was 101–51 in the regular season and 12–4 in the play-offs. I'm proud of the reputations of our teams for turning it up a notch in post-season play. We fight all year to get there, and then we want to see it pay off.

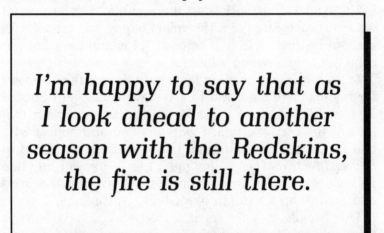

I'm happy to say that as I look ahead to another season with the Redskins, the fire is still there.

I'm happy to say that as I look ahead to another season with the Redskins, the fire is still there. I know I have already had a career a lot of people would be satisfied to retire with, but I'm too young for that. There are more things to do, more goals to accomplish. Most important to me is that I use the platform this job has given me to tell people about what's most important in life. By now you know that I don't think that is football.

That doesn't mean I don't care about the profession that has rewarded me so well. That doesn't mean that I don't care whether we win or lose. I still love winning and hate losing with a passion. I still give every planning session, every practice, every game, and every play all I have to give it. I know what it takes to win, and I won't let up until the day my coaching career is over.

But it is also true that football, just like everything else in this life and this world, is one day going to dry up and blow away. It is not eternal. It is not spiritual. It has many good qualities, but it is not about God and what He should mean to you and me.

There were times in my life when I believed with all my heart that I would not be complete if I didn't get the chance to be a head coach and be able to show people that I could do it. Once I got it, it took on a different perspective. I see the reality of it, the down sides. Don't get me wrong. I believe, with all humility, that I was born to be a football coach. It was my destiny. But it is not and cannot be my end-all in life. If I hadn't gotten my spiritual life straightened out in 1972 and my material life shaken into order by my financial disaster in the 1980s, I might have still thought that becoming a head coach would make me happy.

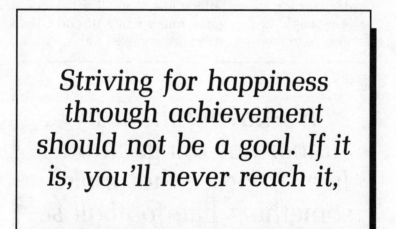

Striving for happiness through achievement should not be a goal. If it is, you'll never reach it,

Striving for happiness through achievement should not be a goal. If it is, you'll never reach it, never attain it. You'll be disappointed and frustrated and maybe even depressed all your life. If I had still been convinced that head coaching would solve all my problems and complete me as a person when I got this job at age forty, I would have been a miserable man. I am happy. I am fulfilled. But it wasn't reaching that plateau that did it. I found another answer. I realized before it was too late that there are more important things in life.

What if I had believed head football coaching was going to do it for me and then I discovered that it didn't change me? It simply brought out the best and the worst in me. I was still the same guy I had always been, but now I had more money and visibility, more responsibility. My life was still hanging in the balance every week, waiting to see if I would feel good and happy because we won, or low and depressed because we lost. That's no way to live. I would have been dejected to the point of despair. You can't pin your hopes and hang your dreams on something so material, so insignificant (sorry, Mr. Cooke).

My boss, and you by now, knows that I do not treat my profession as something trivial. But I'll argue to my dying day that it's having the truly important things in our lives in order that makes something like football so much fun. Too few people in this game really enjoy it, and I think that's because their priorities are screwed up.

> *It's having the truly important things in our lives in order that makes something like football so much fun.*

I don't know what your profession is, but regardless, it has its top rung too, doesn't it? What is your goal? To be president of your company? Top salesman? A teacher or a professor with tenure? Do you want to own your own business? Take it from a guy who knows: Those are all good and worthy goals, but they won't bring you what you really want and need. True success and happiness does not come from material things and dreams coming true. It does not come with achievements. It comes only from knowing God.

Have you noticed on your way up the corporate ladder or on the journey toward the achievement of your goals that no step is totally satisfying? Does it scare you to think that the last big step won't do it for you either? Are you terrified of having to say with the great Peggy Lee, "Is that all there is?"

If you think you're unsatisfied because only the final goal is worthy, you're going to be disappointed. What a tragedy to waste a lifetime on a myth! As I've said, there's nothing wrong with achieving. In fact, a person who belongs to God should strive for nothing but excellence. But set your sights on eternal things, not material.

I'm no preacher or theologian, but I have a few thoughts on what's true and what isn't. If you've been struggling with priorities and dashed hopes and have wondered if there's anything anywhere that can really bring satisfaction, happiness, and a feeling of success, stick with me for one more chapter. You've got nothing to lose; and who knows, you might have everything there is to gain.

Your
Choice

I agree with a lot of people, especially motivational speakers, who like to say that life is like football. We work, we prepare, we struggle, we win, we lose, we have our ups and downs. But my perspective on life and football is from a coach's perspective, not a player's.

For instance, in football, I believe I've had the best situation in the NFL because in Washington I have been one element in a multi-part system required for success. Winning starts with the owner. He is going to decide how much money he's willing to put into the program and how hard you're going to be able to go after what you need. That all depends on his resources and how badly he wants to win.

Then you've got to have another element, the front office. That means a president like John Cooke, who runs the day-to-day operation for his dad, and a general manager who acquires the new talent. Bobby Beathard started me off in Washington, and now we have Charley Casserley doing a fantastic job.

The coaching staff and the fans make up another element. The coaches must have the freedom to make good decisions and motivate the talent. And the fans have to be behind you all the way. Remove any one of those three elements and you're doomed. You'll win a few games, maybe have some decent seasons; but you're not going to be a consistent winner, and you're certainly not going to get to the Super Bowl.

In many ways, life is like that. You have to work with people, and the people in your immediate family—particularly your children—will become your legacy. A godly marriage must have a husband and a wife committed to Jesus Christ. Eliminate any one of those elements and you're as ineffective as an NFL team missing an owner, a president, a G.M., a coaching staff, or loyal fans.

I've been trying to tell you throughout this book that a life spent chasing society's myths will end in frustration. The question is whether that is a lesson that can be learned without living it. You may think it's easy for me to say that climbing the corporate ladder, enjoying personal self-gratifying sports at the expense of your family, making good money, and achieving your dreams is not all it's cracked up to be, because I've done it. Though it is a hard lesson to learn, you may want to learn it yourself. Sure, there are some enjoyable times along the way, but in the end it's not satisfying in itself. People say, "I know money can't buy happiness, but give me a bunch anyway and let me prove it to myself."

If that's where you're coming from, perhaps you can't be convinced. But if you've ever tried to attain success and happiness on your own—without involving the One who made you and loves you—you'll find out sooner or later that I'm right.

Not long ago I read in a daily paper that a major movie star felt a void in his life. I'm talking about a superstar, someone with the world at his feet. He said, "I feel something's missing." No matter how much you accomplish, how much money you make, how many houses and cars you own, or even how many people you entertain, life isn't complete.

Basically, that movie star was saying the same thing I had said most of my life. People who have climbed the same mountains have overdosed on drugs, gone crazy, or just resigned themselves to lives of frustrated misery. They're looking for something only God can give them. He created us with a void that can be filled only with a personal relationship with Him. When we try to fill that void with the things of the world, our bottomless well only gets deeper.

> *Not only will true success elude you when you are seeking happiness on your own, but you will also have no resources when trouble comes.*

Not only will true success elude you when you are seeking happiness on your own, but you will also have no resources when trouble comes. I shudder to think how I would have coped with Pat's surgery, with disastrous seasons, with financial ruin if I hadn't placed my trust in Christ.

If I'm consistent in the faith I've had since I was a child and which I recommitted myself to in Arkansas in 1972, I can rise above circumstances. If God created me special, that means He loves me and cares about me. He's promised that He's in charge. That means I can relax, no matter what goes wrong. I don't always relax, of course, because I'm human and I forget. But I don't have to fight. I can rise above circumstances.

In fact, I should be excited about tough times, because I know God is going to work. I can't say I'd be thrilled if the Redskins lose ten straight and I'm fired, but because of my faith, I should have a bedrock peace about it.

You're never going to get a pro football coach, especially one who belongs to God, to accept losing without hating it. But what I enjoy is a peace about knowing that if everything I do fails, God still loves me. He's still there. He still cares. And He will work it all out for His glory and my good.

That confidence has helped me in coaching. When things turn bad, when you're losing and the criticism mounts, you still want to fight back. You're still competitive. I do everything I can to win, and I'm not lackadaisical or jovial about the process. If we lose, I'm not joking around or acting as if I don't care, because I do care. But my life, my well-being doesn't depend on the win-loss column. I know God has a purpose in adversity and that He will help me rise above it.

People criticize me for working too hard, but I think it's wrong to squander the talents God has given us. I ask a lot from my players and my staff, so I think it's only fair that I do every single thing I can to be prepared. After that, the difference between a coach who has confidence in his faith and one who is living for himself is that I can live with the outcome, regardless. I may not like it, but I can leave it with God.

I'll never easily accept defeat, but once I have done all I can do, I find it easier to leave it in God's hands. If it didn't work, if I was a coach who lost more than he won, then you'd have to wonder if my faith made me soft and too accepting of hardship. The difference is not in preparation or approach. The difference is in reacting to the result.

I disagree with football players who believe in Christ and think that means they should be softer, less aggressive. They're wrong. They're not taking their profession seriously enough. That makes me mad. The believer has more reason than anyone to be the best. Football is an aggressive game and some of the most aggressive people I've ever met are Christian football players. If you've been given a gift, whether as a player or a coach, you have an obligation to make the absolute most of that.

> *I disagree with football players who believe in Christ and think that means they should be softer, less aggressive. They're wrong.*

So, the message I want to get across to you? If you've gotten nothing from this book except a few laughs and a lot of football, I have wasted my time and yours. I want you to have a right relationship with the Lord. That's the real value in life, that's the real treasure. If you live by the world's standard, as I did for so many years, and you try to achieve something by making money and winning football games, you're going to find yourself at forty and fifty and sixty having missed the real important thing: the influence you can have on others that will last for eternity.

Someday it will dawn on you that the world has passed off a hoax on you—that at the end of the journey toward self-fulfillment, there's nothing. The bill of goods was worthless. The promise is not true. What an awful discovery!

Winning Super Bowls has been great, exhilarating, thrilling. I won't kid you. But even more dynamic to me was hugging and kissing first J.D. in 1983 and Coy in 1988 when those games were over. They were my boys, my family, the product of my love for Pat. I had learned to carve out time for them and to make helping them and others more important than making a name for myself.

Run from that myth that material success will bring you happiness. And ignore its counterpart, the lie that the world loves you. The crowd loves a football coach when he succeeds on the fourth and one call they were screaming for. But where are they when it fails, when the team loses, when you've made a mistake that puts a ballgame out of reach? That's when you learn what the world really thinks of you. They love you as long as you deliver for them. Is the Joe Gibbs who calls the right play a different guy from the Joe Gibbs who calls for a screen pass deep in his own territory with time running out in the first half of a Super Bowl? Of course not. But one is revered and the other is booed. One is a genius, the other a buffoon. That's the consistency of the love of the world. Cast your lot with the God in whom there is no change, neither shadow of turning. He loves you as much when you're on the bottom as when you're on top, and it's even clearer and more real to you when you're suffering.

I've walked anonymously into a restaurant and been treated like a dog. Then they recognize me and all of a sudden I'm worthy of the best seat in the house. Let others wait. That is discrimination. That is unfair. That is fickle. Who was I when you didn't know I was coach of the Redskins? Compare that with the unconditional love of God.

The last myth that needs to be trashed is the one that says that this life is all there is. You only go around once, so grab all the gusto you can. That might make for an entertaining beer commercial, but making it your philosophy of life doesn't even make sense. Would a personal God who made you special and who cares about you and loves you unconditionally leave you on this earth to live a life of frustration and emptiness?

I wondered about that for a long time. What was the alternative to all this struggling for success and happiness and things? I found the answer. It lies in having a personal relationship with Christ. God sent Him to live a perfect life and die for our sins. He came back to life and through him we have the path to God. All you have to do is believe in Him and receive Him into your life. The decision is yours.

I know that by saying this, by putting it in my book, I

open myself to criticism. There will be reviewers and sportswriters and maybe even fans who will say that all this religious talk has no place in a football coach's book. But it's my story. It's my life. It's what really matters to me. So, even if you don't agree with it, and even if you're offended by it, I couldn't have done a book and left it out.

Learn from my mistakes. I've tried to be vulnerable and honest. Look at how God has guided me in spite of my stupid blunders. He's always there. He wants a relationship with you. If you've never had that, let me do here what I do when I speak: give you a sample prayer that God promises to answer if you say it to Him sincerely.

Just pray: "Dear God, I know I'm a sinner. Thank You for sending Your Son, Jesus Christ, to die for my sins. I accept Your forgiveness and receive Him into my life. Thank You for saving me and promising me eternity with You when I die. In the name of Jesus, Amen."

If you've ever prayed that prayer and meant it, you're on the way to true success. Get into a good church and study the Bible. It promises that the Bible " . . . shall not depart from your mouth, but you shall meditate in it day and night, that you may observe to do according to all that is written in it. For then you will make your way prosperous, *and then you will have good success*" (Josh. 1:8, emphasis added).

That's quite a promise. Prosperity and good success in the best senses of those words await you if you study God's Word.

Without Christ, my life would be nothing. It would be an exercise in futility. I would be working day and night for things that will wind up in the trash can. You can live your life and end up leaving this earth forever separated from God and having your life count for nothing more than the money you've made or the goals you've achieved, or you can put your trust in the One who can make your life really count.

This life is not all there is. You're going to live forever. The question is where and with whom? Christ is the answer, and even if saying so sacrifices some sales of this book, it's the message I want you to get. I've shared my story so you might avoid my mistakes and do the one right thing I have done in my life: Turn it over to Jesus Christ.

You can say yes, I'll do that . . . or no, I won't. But make a decision. Because no decision is a No decision. You're risking everything. I pray you'll receive Christ. And if you do, I'd love to hear from you.

Afterword: The Road to Super Bowl XXVI

Joe Gibbs was privately high on his 1991 version of the Washington Redskins. He liked the core of veteran players—"the older guys," he called them—who had been with him since his first Super Bowl win in January of 1983. Center Jeff Bostic, tackle Joe Jacoby, tight end Don Warren, guard Russ Grimm, and linebacker Monte Coleman led by example all season. They played as if they might never have another chance for that rare Super Bowl ring.

Quarterback Mark Rypien, who had done so much and been so maligned by critics, couldn't come to terms with the Redskins on an extended contract and even held out for a time, finally agreeing on a one-year deal. That would prove costly for the Redskins, because there is nothing more expensive than a player whose contract has expired and who reigns as the most effective player in the game at his position when it's all over.

The tight-knit group of friends and compatriots that had made up the nucleus of Joe Gibbs's coaching staff for a decade believed they had a 1991 team with few holes. This was not a swaggering, big-talking staff. Like their leader, they were quiet, self-effacing, hard-working, hours-logging tacticians who believed in covering all the bases. Even the players commented they felt conspicuous if they cut corners, because they knew the coaches were devoting every walking moment to the success of the team.

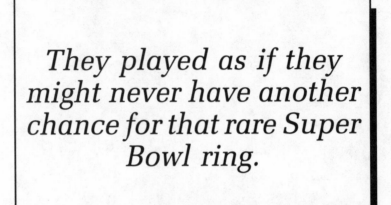

They played as if they might never have another chance for that rare Super Bowl ring.

The pre-season favorites to go to the January 1992 Super Bowl were, as expected, the previous year's combatants: the defending champion New York Giants and the heartbroken 20–19 losers, the Buffalo Bills. A missed field goal in the final seconds had meant the difference in Super Bowl XXV. Late in the 1991 season, when the Giants fell on hard times and the Bills had roared to a 10–1 mark, the Bills were viewed as likely to avenge their Super Bowl defeat. Buffalo had averaged an incredible 31 points in those first 11 games.

But the Redskins had jumped to their best start ever, winning all of their first eleven contests while averaging nearly 33 points per game. Already pundits pointed to the inevitable Bills-Redskins showdown in Super Bowl XXVI, saying that any two lesser opponents would be anti-climactic. The Redskins had shutout three of their first five opponents and would hold five teams to single digits over the 16-game season. The Bills would allow 94 more points during the season, while still holding opponents to an average of fewer than 20 per game. The Skins held their opponents to an average of 14.

In their twelfth game of the season, the Redskins dropped a home game 24–21 to arch-rival Dallas, then beat the Rams and the Cardinals on the road before toppling the defending champion Giants for the second time, 34–17. Washington lost its final game of the regular season at Philadelphia, 24–22, in an otherwise meaningless game. Meanwhile, their collision-course buddies, the Bills, lost at New England, beat the Jets, the Raiders, and the Colts, and lost the season finale 17–14 at home against Detroit.

In the divisional playoffs, Buffalo (13–3) had little trouble with Kansas City, winning 37–14, while the Redskins (14–2) beat Atlanta 24–7. For the American Football Conference championship, Buffalo outlasted Denver 10–7 in a brutal defensive game. Denver had come back to win over Houston in their semi-final game on a dramatic charge led by veteran quarterback John Elway. The Broncos were desperate to return to the Super Bowl, having lost in all four of their appearances, including three in the last five years. But Buffalo's defense was too much for them.

The Redskins had to play the hottest team in the NFL, the Detroit Lions, who had gone undefeated at home and had surprised everyone by upsetting the Chicago Bears to win the central division. Their coach, Wayne Fontes, would be named NFL Coach of the Year, and despite the fact that Washington had opened the season with a 45–0 thrashing of the Lions, some prognosticators gave the momentum and destiny edge to Detroit for the NFC championship.

Mike Utley of Detroit, who had become a national focus of attention when he had been paralyzed in an earlier game, had also become a rallying point for the Lions. He had been able to flash a thumbs-up sign as he was wheeled from the field after his injury, and that signal became symbolic for the upstart Lions. The players flashed it frequently and dedicated the season to their injured teammate. But in a game that should have indicated to the Bills that emotion, momentum, and destiny mean less than skill and execution, the Redskins easily dominated the Lions 41–10. In a gesture of sportsmanship, the Redskins adopted the thumbs-up sign to carry the Mike Utley spirit into the Super Bowl.

> *The Redskins adopted the thumbs-up sign to carry the Mike Utley spirit into the Super Bowl.*

With two weeks between the AFC and NFC championships and the Super Bowl in Minneapolis, the Bills and the Redskins had time to recover from nagging injuries and fully prepare for the game of games. That also gave the media time to hype the Super Bowl past all logic. Only ten Super Bowls have been decided by ten or fewer points, and six of the previous eight could be considered boring blowouts. But now the experts were saying they finally had a match-up worthy of the ballyhoo. Though the Redskins were favored by at least a touchdown, many were picking the Bills. The Skins were considered boring and methodical, a machine with parts and a tactical coaching staff. The Bills were a team of stars, of offensive weapons, of personalities. And they were on a mission. While Washington would be making its fourth appearance in ten years and fifth overall, the Bills' one-point loss the previous year was still a fresh wound. Ten Super Bowl winners had been previous Super Bowl losers. Only seven first time Super Bowl teams had won it.

Jim Kelly, the Bills' handsome quarterback, was seen as a media darling, the kind of guy who could really cash in if the Bills won. Thurman Thomas, their 1,400-yard rusher and NFL MVP, was a brash talking, dozen-touchdown producing man who complained he had been overlooked by the media. He claimed he and Kelly should be considered the Michael Jordans of the Bills.

While Washington clearly had the edge on defense, their season scoring edge was just 485–458. Still, the game seemed a toss up to many. Buffalo had a nerve-racking no-huddle offense that had riddled defenses for two years.

Most gave the quarterback edge to Buffalo because Kelly had been to the Super Bowl before. In fact, Kelly interviewed Rypien on his talk show during Super Bowl week and concluded that Rypien was as overwhelmed with the media coverage as Kelly had been the year before.

The running backs edge also went to Buffalo because of Thurman Thomas. He had led the NFL in combined rushing and receiving yardage for the third straight season. There may have also been a slight edge to the Bills on the defensive line, but after that it was all Washington. Receivers, offensive line, linebackers, secondary, special teams, and coaching all had to lean toward the Skins. Gibbs brought an incredible 16–4 post-season record into the game, including a 2–1 Super Bowl mark.

Gary Clark, Art Monk, and Ricky Sanders—the Washington receivers known as The Posse—were the best in the game. Coach Joe Gibbs knew, however, that Buffalo's Andre Reed, James Lofton, and Don Beebe were not far behind. And with Thomas and end Keith McKeller, the Bills may have brought more balance into the game.

The edge for kicker had to go to Chip Lohmiller of the Redskins. He had kicked for the University of Minnesota, so he would be at home in the Hubert H. Humphrey Metrodome. Buffalo's Scott Norwood wanted to avenge his late fourth-quarter miss in the previous Super Bowl that had cost the Bills the game, but Lohmiller had outscored him 149–110 during the regular season.

As Super Sunday drew closer, the media blitz intensified until all that was left to talk about were the technical details of the CBS telecast, the statistics, and the dollars.

A 30-second block of commercial time was going for $850,000. Sixty-three thousand one-hundred and thirty people would see the game live. Winners would claim $36,000 per player; losers, half that.

The Bills took on the persona of a team with a chip on its shoulder. Gibbs and the Redskins appeared looser, but the coach maintained a low profile. Following his lead, the players refused to brag or predict victory. They gave the Bills their due, admitted that anybody could be beaten on a given day, and expressed concern over the many strengths Buffalo would bring to the game.

The Bills predicted victory. "We don't get the respect we deserve," they said. "But that's OK. We don't mind earning it." Thurman Thomas put the onus on himself. "As I go, so goes the offense. If I struggle, we're going to struggle." Bills' linebacker Cornelius Bennett told reporters, "This time around, we're going to win. We know now what it takes to win this kind of a game."

Fans settled into the Metrodome hours before kickoff, and Super Bowl parties moved into high gear all over the country. The pre-game shows droned on, trying to add drama and excitement to a game that should have provided its own. The match-up was a football fan's dream. Washington quarterback Mark Rypien said, "What more could the NFL want? Two teams that have finished tops in the game going at it. Strength against strength." It would be the first time that the two clearly best teams had wound up facing each other at the end of the season since 1984. That was the year the San Francisco Forty-Niners whipped the Miami Dolphins 38–16.

Gibbs believed his team had few holes and was as prepared as it could be. "I do think anyone could beat us though," he said.

Buffalo coach Marv Levy didn't even want to talk about defeat. "We would be sorely disappointed," he said.

By game time, 5:18 p.m., CDT, the talk and the hyperbole were over. The game would be decided on the field.

Neither team looked impressive in the first quarter. Scott Norwood misunderstood the official's signal asking if he was ready for the opening kickoff. Rather than waiting for the official to see if the Redskins were ready, Norwood kicked off. His kick had sailed all the way out of the endzone. Unfortunately for him, the boot was called back. His re-kick was not as good, but the Redskins had trouble moving the ball and had to punt.

When the Bills took over, their MVP was not on the field for the first two plays. Someone had moved Thurman Thomas's helmet, and he was scurrying to find it. By the time he joined his team, it was third and long, and Kelly was about to be sacked.

The Redskins moved the ball better. After eventually moving to the Bills' two-yard-line, Rypien hit Art Monk with an apparent touchdown pass in the back of the endzone. For the first time in the history of the Super Bowl, the play was called back after an instant replay review when it was clear Monk's trailing foot came down out of bounds. It appeared Monk might have been forced out of the endzone by the defender, but Washington didn't protest. Unable to punch the ball into the endzone, the Skins lined up for a 19-yard field goal attempt, a virtual chip shot for a kicker like Lohmiller. But the snap sailed through the hands of holder Jeff Rutledge, and Gibbs had to be wondering how many blown opportunities his team could get away with in a game of this magnitude and against an opponent as potent as the Bills.

When Kelly and Rypien threw interceptions on consecutive possessions, the game began to look like a Super Bust. It would be the first time in fifteen years that the first quarter of a Super Bowl ended in a scoreless tie. Less than two minutes into the second period, however, Washington drove deep into Buffalo territory when Earnest Byner ran for 19 yards and Rypien hit Ricky Sanders with a 41-yard pass. Lohmiller lined up for a field goal from 34 yards. Ironically, the snap and hold were shaky, but Rutledge and Lohmiller made it work, giving their team a 3–0 lead.

Three minutes later Washington had driven 51 yards in

five plays to the Bills' 10-yard line. Rypien had connected with Gary Clark on a 16-yard pass, and the Bills had lost ten more yards on a roughing-the-passer call against Cornelius Bennett. When Rypien found Byner in the endzone and Lohmiller added the extra point, the Skins were up 10-0 with about ten minutes to play in the half.

Less than three minutes later the Redskins struck again. Rypien hit Clark with a 34-yard pass, and Ricky Ervins scampered 14 yards to the Buffalo one-yard line. Gerald Riggs, who had led Washington with 11 touchdowns during the regular season, plunged into the endzone, Lohmiller added the extra point, and suddenly things looked bleak for the Bills.

The Washington defense was swarming and blitzing, and because the Bills were down 17-0, they couldn't afford to stay with the run. Thurman Thomas would complain later that he had been underused, and his ten carries for 13 yards in the game would be one of his least productive performances ever.

In the locker room at the half, the Bills having become the first Super Bowl team to be held scoreless in the first half since game number XVI, Coach Levy told his players they had the chance to stage the biggest upset in the history of the contest. Sixteen seconds into the second half, however, the Redskins virtually put the game away. Linebacker Kurt Gouveia intercepted a Kelly pass and returned it 23 yards. Two plays later Riggs crashed in from the two, Lohmiller kicked the PAT, and it was 24–0 Washington.

Buffalo came back with a 77-yard, 11-play drive, including a 14-yard pass from Kelly to James Lofton and a 43-yard pass from Kelly to Don Beebe, but the Bills had to settle for a 21-yard field goal by Norwood. With six minutes to go in the quarter, the Bills finally scored a touchdown. On a muffed play and a pass interference call, they had reached the Washington one-yard line before Thomas ran it in and Norwood added the extra point. Now the Bills were within two touchdowns at 24–10.

Four-and-a-half minutes later, Rypien had led the Redskins to the Buffalo 30 in ten plays, including passes of 10 and 14 yards to Clark. Then Rypien hit Clark with a touchdown pass, Lohmiller did his thing, and it was 31–10.

In the opening seconds of the fourth period, defensive end Fred Stokes recovered a Kelly fumble on the Bills' 14, and though the Redskins could manage only seven yards in four plays, Lohmiller booted a 25-yard field goal to make the margin 34–10. Three minutes later, after Brad Edwards's 35-yard interception return and Ervins's 14-yard run, Lohmiller added a 39-yard field goal to put the game out of reach at 37–10.

Buffalo scored on two more Kelly TD passes to make the game look closer than it really was at 37–24. The second TD came after a successful but controversial onside kick that appeared to have been touched by Buffalo before it had traveled the required ten yards.

But there was not enough time for Buffalo to mount a serious challenge after that, and the dominant team of the 1991 regular season had made a rout of another Super Bowl. Mark Rypien was named MVP after throwing two TD passes and enjoying the kind of protection a quarterback dreams about. Most impressive, the Redskins made more use of the no-huddle offense than the Bills had, and even more than the Skins had throughout the season. Lohmiller had kicked three field goals and four extra points, and Washington had scored 20 points after Buffalo turnovers. It was the eighth NFC Super Bowl in nine years.

The Bills had tried intimidating the Skins' receivers—Clark, Sanders, and Monk—glaring and pointing at them after particularly good hits. But Clark gained 114 yards anyway, and Monk 113. "I don't even let my mom stare at me," Clark said, "let alone anybody else."

Marv Levy was as disappointed as he predicted he would be. "I kept hoping we would pull out a miracle finish," he said. "We came into the game extremely well prepared. It was tough enough to lose to the Giants last year, but this was even worse. I can't see how we could have worked any harder or with any more intensity. The harder you work, the harder it is to surrender."

Kelly was sacked five times and finished with 28 completions in a record 58 throws. He was intercepted four times. Once he was nearly knocked out. He complained after the game that he could remember little of what went on. "What I do remember I don't like," he said.

The post-game attention, of course, turned to the Redskins and their veteran head coach. Joe Gibbs took several media opportunities to shared the credit with his players, his management, and his coaching staff. He said he was humbled because he knew he would get a lot of credit for things he didn't do—or certainly didn't do alone. "The Lord has blessed me with a great situation," he said frequently.

Because other celebrated head coaches of Super Bowl winners, like Bill Walsh of the Forty-Niners and Bill Parcells of the Giants, had retired after their biggest and most satisfying victories, there was speculation about Gibbs. What could be more fulfilling than winning three of four Super Bowls in ten years? Was there anything left to accomplish? Could he still deny he was one of the great tacticians in the game with that kind of a record? In 1982 when the press had called him a genius, he demurred, saying, "Let's see if I'm standing here in ten years." He was, for the third time in four tries. So are there no more mountains to climb? Is there a lucrative commentator deal on the horizon that will give him a break from the stressful, wall-to-wall schedule he lives with during the season?

Not a chance, says Gibbs. "I have no thoughts about stepping away from this. We'll tee it up and try to do it again next year."

Jerry Jenkins
January 26, 1992

SUPER BOWL XXVI SCORING SUMMARY

Washington	0	17	14	6—37
Buffalo	0	0	10	14—24

■ First Quarter

—Scoreless

■ Second quarter

—FG Lohmiller 34, 1:58. Drive: 64 yards, 7 plays. Washington 3, Buffalo 0

—Byner 10 pass from Rypien (Lohmiller kick), 5:06. Drive: 51 yards, 5 plays. Washington 10, Buffalo 0.

—Riggs 1 run (Lohmiller kick), 7:43. Drive: 55 yards, 5 plays. Washington 17, Buffalo 0.

■ Third quarter

—Riggs 2 run (Lohmiller kick), :16. Drive: 2 yards, 1 play. Washington 24, Buffalo 0.

—FG Norwood 21, 3:01. Drive: 77 yards, 11 plays. Washington 24, Buffalo 3.

—Thomas 1 run (Norwood kick), 9:02. Drive: 56 yards, 6 plays. Washington 24, Buffalo 10.

—Clark 30 pass from Rypien (Lohmiller kick), 13:36. Drive: 79 yards, 11 plays. Washington 31, Buffalo 10.

■ Fourth quarter

—FG Lohmiller 25, :06. Drive: 7 yards, 4 plays. Washington 34, Buffalo 10.

—FG Lohmiller 39, 3:24. Drive: 11 yards, 5 plays. Washington 37, Buffalo 10.

—Metzelaars 2 pass from Kelly (Norwood kick), 9:01. Drive: 79 yards, 15 plays. Washington 37, Buffalo 17.

—Beebe 4 pass from Kelly (Norwood kick), 11:05. Drive: 50 yards, 9 plays. Washington 37, Buffalo 24.

A—63,130. No-shows—None.

Category	Wash.	Buffalo
First downs	24	25
Rushing	10	4
Passing	12	18
Penalty	2	3
Third down eff	6-16	7-17
Fourth down eff	0-1	2-2
Total net yards	417	283
Total plays	73	82
Avg gain	5.7	3.5
Net yards rushing	125	43
Rushes	40	18
Avg per rush	3.1	2.4
Net yards passing	292	240
Completed-att.	18-33	29-59
Yards per pass	8.8	3.8
Sacked-yds lost	0-0	5-46
Had intercepted	1	4
Punts-avg.	4-37	6-35
Had blocked	0	0
Total return yards	95	90
Punt returns	0-0	3-9
Kickoff returns	1-16	4-77
Interceptions	4-79	1-4
Penalties-yds	5-82	6-50
Fumbles-lost	1-0	6-1
Time of possession	33:43	26:17

Individual statistics

Rushing: WASHINGTON: Ervins 13-72, Byner 14-49, Riggs 5-7, Sanders 1-1, Rutledge 1-0, Rypien 6-(-4). BUFFALO: Davis 4-17, Kelly 3-16, Thomas 10-13, Lofton 1-(-3).

Passing: WASHINGTON: Rypien 18-33-292-2-1. BUFFALO: Kelly 28-58-275-2-4; Reich 1-1-11-0-11-0.

Receiving: WASHINGTON; Clark 7-114, Monk 7-113, Byner 3-24, Sanders 1-41. BUFFALO: Lofton 7-92, Reed 5-

34, Beebe 4-61, Davis 4-38, Thomas 4-27, McKeller 2-29, A. Edwards 1-11, Metzelaars 1-2, Kelly 1-(-8).

Tackles-Solos-Assists: WASHINGTON: Marshall 8-3-1; Mayhew 6-0-0; Stokes 5-1-1; Collins 5-0-0; T. Johnson 3-2-0; Mays 3-1-1; B. Edwards 3-1-0; Gouveia 3-1-0; Geathers 2-1-1; Green 2-0-0; Hoage 2-0-0; Caldwell 2-0-0; Hobbs 2-0-0; Buck 1-0-1; S. Johnson 1-0-0; Coleman 1-0-0; E. Williams 1-0-0; Lohmiller 1-0-0; Jacoby 1-0-0; Mann 0-1-0; Rutledge 0-0-0. BUFFALO: Bailey 7-4-0; Bennett 6-1-0; Talley 5-3-0; Jackson 5-0-0; Kelso 4-2-0; Seals 3-3-0; Odomes 3-1-0; Drane 3-1-0; Bentley 3-0-0; Wright 2-1-0; B. Smith 2-0-0; Garner 2-0-0; J. Williams 1-0-0; Jones 1-0-0; Thomas 1-0-0; Richter 1-0-0; Lofton 1-0-0; Kelly 0-0-0; Ballard 0-0-0.

Missed field goals: None.

Time: 3:43.

1991 SEASON AND SUPER BOWL STATISTICS

1991 Regular Season
Won 14, lost 2

Wash		Opp
45	Detroit	0
33	at Dallas	31
34	Phoenix	0
34	at Cincinnati	27
23	Philadelphia	0
20	at Bears	7
42	Cleveland	17
17	at NY Giants	13
16	Houston-x	13
56	Atlanta	17
41	at Pittsburgh	14
21	Dallas	24
27	at Rams	6
20	at Phoenix	14
34	NY Giants	17
22	at Philadelphia	24

Divisional playoff
Washington 24, Atlanta 7
NFC Championship
Washington 41, Detroit 10
Super Bowl XXVI
Washington 37, Buffalo 24

(x—Overtime)

Super Bowl MVPs

'67: Bart Starr, QB, Green Bay
'68: Bart Starr, QB, Green Bay
'69: Joe Namath, QB, NY Jets
'70: Len Dawson, QB, Kansas City
'71: Chuck Howley, LB, Dallas
'72: Roger Staubach, QB, Dallas
'73: Jake Scott, S, Miami
'74: Larry Csonka, RB, Miami
'75: Franco Harris, RB, Pittsburgh
'76: Lynn Swann, WR, Pittsburgh
'77: Fred Biletnikoff, WR, Oakland
'78: Randy White, DT, and Harvey
    Martin, DE, Dallas
'79: Terry Bradshaw, QB, Pittsburgh
'80: Terry Bradshaw, QB, Pittsburgh
'81: Jim Plunkett, QB, Oakland
'82: Joe Montana, QB, San Francisco
'83: John Riggins, RB, Washington
'84: Marcus Allen, RB, LA Raiders
'85: Joe Montana, QB, San Francisco
'86: Richard Dent, DE, Chicago
'87: Phil Simms, QB, NY Giants
'88: Doug Williams, QB, Washington
'89: Jerry Rice, WR, San Francisco
'90: Joe Montana, QB, San Francisco
'91: Otis Anderson, RB, NY Giants
'92: Mark Rypien, QB, Washington

Year-by-Year Super Bowl Results

Year	Winner	Loser
1967	Green Bay (NFL) 35	Kansas City (AFL) 10
1968	Green Bay (NFL) 33	Oakland (AFL) 14
1969	NY Jets (AFL) 16	Baltimore (NFL) 7
1970	Kansas City (AFL) 23	Minnesota (NFL) 7
1971	Baltimore (AFC) 16	Dallas (NFC) 13
1972	Dallas (NFC) 24	Miami (AFC) 3
1973	Miami (AFC) 14	Washington (NFC) 7
1974	Miami (AFC) 24	Minnesota (NFC) 7
1975	Pittsburgh (AFC) 16	Minnesota (NFC) 6
1976	Pittsburgh (AFC) 21	Dallas (NFC) 17
1977	Oakland (AFC) 32	Minnesota (NFC) 14
1978	Dallas (NFC) 27	Denver (AFC) 10
1979	Pittsburgh (AFC) 35	Dallas (NFC) 31
1980	Pittsburgh (AFC) 31	Los Angeles (NFC) 19
1981	Oakland (AFC) 27	Philadelphia (NFC) 10
1982	San Francisco (NFC) 26	Cincinnati (AFC) 21
1983	Washington (NFC) 27	Miami (AFC) 17
1984	L.A. Raiders (AFC) 38	Washington (NFC) 9
1985	San Francisco (NFC) 38	Miami (AFC) 16
1986	Chicago (NFC) 46	New England (AFC) 10
1987	NY Giants (NFC) 39	Denver (AFC) 20
1988	Washington (NFC) 42	Denver (AFC) 10
1989	San Francisco (NFC) 20	Cincinnati (AFC) 16
1990	San Francisco (NFC) 55	Denver (AFC) 10
1991	NY Giants (NFC) 20	Buffalo (AFC) 19
1992	Washington (NFC) 37	Buffalo (AFC) 24

Career Statistics

11 YEARS WITH GIBBS—Joe Gibbs ended his 11th season in Washington and boasts a 115–53–0 (.685) regular season mark. He is 130–57–0 (.695) overall, including a 15–4–0 (.789) play-off record.

Gibbs is the third winningest coach among active NFL coaches, trailing only Don Shula and Chuck Knox.

Gibbs also moved up to 12th place all-time with his 130-career victories.

GIBBS IN THE PLAY-OFFS—In Gibbs' 11 seasons, there have been seven play-off berths, five division titles, five NFC championship appearances, four Super Bowl trips and three world titles.

The Skins are 15–4 (.789) under Gibbs in the play-offs, which is the second-best winning percentage among active NFL coaches.

His 15 play-off wins are the second most among active NFL coaches (with Don Shula winning 17). And among coaches with 100 career victories, Gibbs has the third best mark in NFL history:

Coach	Team(s)	Postseason Record	
Vince Lombardi	Packers	9–1–0	.900
Weeb Ewbank	Colts, Jets	4–1–0	.800
Joe Gibbs	Redskins	15–4–0	.789
Buddy Parker	Lions	3–1–0	.750

REDSKINS IN POSTSEASON UNDER JOE GIBBS

1982 Redskins 31 Lions 7   (Play-off, 1/8/83)
    Redskins 21 Vikings 7   (Play-off, 1/15/83)
    Redskins 31 Cowboys 17 (NFC Championship, 1/22/83)
    Redskins 27 Dolphins 17 (Super Bowl XVII, 1/30/83)

1983	Redskins 51 Rams 7	(Divisional Play-off, 1/1/84)
	Redskins 24 49ers 21	(NFC Championship, 1/8/84)
	Raiders 38 Redskins 9	(Super Bowl XVIII, 1/22/84)
1984	Bears 23 Redskins 19	(Divisional Play-off, 12/30/84)
1986	Redskins 19 Rams 7	(Wild Card Play-off, 12/28/86)
	Redskins 27 Bears 13	(Divisional Play-off, 1/3/87)
	Giants 17 Redskins 0	(NFC Championship, 1/11/87)
1987	Redskins 21 Bears 17	(Divisional Play-off, 1/10/88)
	Redskins 17 Vikings 10	(NFC Championship, 1/17/88)
	Redskins 42 Broncos 10	(Super Bowl XXII, 1/31/88)
1990	Redskins 20 Eagles 6	(Wild Card Play-off, 1/5/91)
	49ers 28 Redskins 10	(Divisional Play-off, 1/12/91)
1991	Redskins 24 Falcons 7	(Divisional Play-off, 1/4/92)
	Redskins 41 Lions 10	(NFC Championship, 1/12/92)
	Redskins 37 Bills 24	(Super Bowl XXVI, 1/26/92)

About the Authors

Joe Gibbs began his coaching career in 1964 as an assistant coach at San Diego State where he had previously played under Coach Don Coryell. Gibbs later held coaching positions at Florida State, USC, and Arkansas before entering the pro ranks as offensive backfield coach for the St. Louis Cardinals from 1973–77. After a season with the Tampa Bay Buccaneers, Gibbs joined the San Diego Chargers as offensive coordinator in 1979. In 1981, Gibbs joined the Washington Redskins as head coach.

Originally from North Carolina, Gibbs lives outside Washington, D.C., with his wife, Pat, and their two sons: J.D. and Coy.

If you desire additional information on how to receive Christ as your personal Savior, please write Joe Gibbs in care of Columbia Baptist Church, 103 West Columbia Street, Falls Church, Virginia 22046. If you want to know more about what God has to say about your money, mention that in your letter and Joe will send you more information.

Jerry Jenkins is a widely published author of biographies and fiction. He has written the biographies of Orel Hershiser (on the *New York Times* Bestseller List for nine weeks), Mike Singletary, Meadowlark Lemon, Hank Aaron, Walter Payton, B.J. Thomas, Sammy Tippit, George Sweeting, and Luis Palau.

Jenkins is writer-in-residence at Moody Bible Institute. Born in Kalamazoo, Michigan, Jenkins lives near Zion, Illinois, with his wife, Dianna, and their three sons: Dallas, Chad, and Michael.

If you desire additional information on how to receive Christ as your personal Savior, please write Joe Gibbs in care of Columbia Baptist Church, 103 West Columbia Street, Falls Church, Virginia 22046. If you want to know more about what God has to say about your money, mention that in your letter and Joe will send you more information.